# HOW TO TALK TO ANYONE

## A STEP-BY-STEP GUIDE TO TACKLE SOCIAL ANXIETY, STRENGTHEN RELATIONSHIPS, ELEVATE COMMUNICATION SKILLS, AND THRIVE IN EVERY SETTING

C. HOLMBAECK AND R. ESKILDSEN

First edition published by
C. Holmbaeck and R. Eskildsen, 2024
Copyright© 2024 by C. Holmbaeck
Paperback: ISBN 978-87-975579-0-7
Hardcover: ISBN 978-87-975579-1-4



**This book is intended for informational and guidance purposes only**
The content in "How to Talk to Anyone" is based on the authors research, experiences, and opinions, and is not meant to replace professional advice or therapy. Readers are encouraged to consult relevant professionals in psychology, communication, or other fields if specific guidance or assistance is needed.

**Individual results may vary**
The advice and techniques presented in this book are designed to enhance everyday communication and build better relationships, but the effectiveness of these methods may vary depending on individual circumstances and context. No guarantees are provided that the described methods will result in specific outcomes for the reader.

**The authors and publishers disclaim any liability for unintended consequences**
The application of the advice and methods presented in this book is at the reader's own discretion. The authors and publishers cannot be held liable for any form of harm, loss, or discomfort that may arise from the use of the content.

**This book is not a substitute for professional help**
If the reader experiences significant challenges in their relationships, communication, or mental health, it is recommended to seek professional help from a qualified therapist, psychologist, or counselor.

# TABLE OF CONTENTS

## Chapter 5
## Strengthen Relationships with the 5 Love Languages

# INTRODUCTION

Communication isn't just about sharing information—it's about building relationships with others. As we develop and improve our conversational skills, we positively impact both our personal and professional lives. We can form strong connections where we both understand and feel understood. Clear and empathetic communication helps us forge deeper bonds with loved ones, improve collaboration with colleagues, and boost our confidence in social situations.

When we invest time and energy into improving our communication, we also invest in our well-being and the relationships that matter most to us.

This book will begin by laying a solid foundation, focusing on building confidence in social settings and addressing challenges like shyness and social anxiety. Then, we'll explore the psychological aspects of communication, examining how our voice, tone, and body language influence our messages. We will introduce you to techniques for engaging in conversations, building solid connections, and navigating specific situations with friends, family, spouses, and colleagues. We'll move on to practical strategies for handling criticism, establishing and respecting personal boundaries, and de-escalating conflicts. Finally, we'll dive into the love languages, which apply to all close relationships, and provide tools to strengthen your bonds through understanding and applying these concepts.

Each chapter has practical examples and exercises, making applying the new principles in your daily life easy. No matter where you start or what your goals are, this book will guide you on your journey to becoming a more confident and effective communicator.

## Strengthen Your Communication with a Journal

If you aim to improve your communication skills, we encourage you to develop your personal communication strategy based on this book's theories and practical suggestions. Your plan should align with your unique needs and goals, considering your experiences and challenges. You can create your strategy by selecting the most resonating methods and techniques from the book. When you focus on what genuinely interests you, you'll be far more motivated to practice, and this will help you reach your goals and achieve the growth you desire.

An essential part of your strategy could be using a journal to document your experiences, challenges, and successes. Writing down your observations and experiences—whether in a journal, on your phone, in a notebook, or in another format that works best for you—makes it easier to reflect on your progress. By choosing a format you're comfortable with, you'll find it easier to adapt and refine your strategy, as confidence is a skill you can develop with time, patience, and practice.

By following the suggestions and exercises presented in this book, you can systematically work toward your communication goals. Your journal will serve as a record of your growth and a valuable tool for reflecting and adjusting your strategies. This process will help you achieve your goals and build lasting skills in effective communication.

## From us to you
# PRINTABLE REFLECTION CARDS AND CHECKLISTS

To help you put the book's content into practice, we've designed 50 reflection cards and 6 checklists for you to download and print.

The purpose of these reflection cards is to support your personal growth and strengthen your relationships through small, daily tasks and reflections. The checklists provide a practical way to track your progress and help you reach your goals.

You can download the reflection cards and checklists by scanning the QR code below:

Happy reading,
C. Holmbaeck and
R. Eskildsen

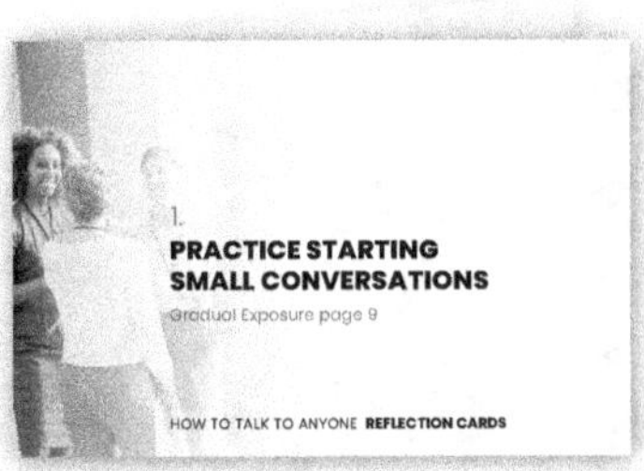

# Chapter 1:

# BUILDING CONFIDENCE IN SOCIAL SETTINGS

No matter why you've chosen to read this book, there's one thing we all have in common: the desire to become better communicators and feel comfortable in social situations. Perhaps you seek practical advice to improve your conversations and build stronger relationships. Or maybe you're generally shy and long for the confidence that makes engaging in discussions and social gatherings easier. For some, social anxiety may be a challenge, and even everyday social situations feel overwhelming.

Confidence is not just about feeling comfortable and being willing to try new approaches in our conversations with others; it's about expressing our thoughts and feelings in a way that captures the attention of others.

When we confidently communicate, our words carry weight, our body language supports our message, and our intent is clear and convincing. This alignment is crucial, as it directly impacts how others perceive and respond to us, whether we're giving a presentation at work or chatting with a friend at a café. The confidence behind our words shapes the dynamic of the conversation.

## Shyness and Social Anxiety

Shyness and social anxiety can make speaking with others and participating in social settings difficult. Shyness is a familiar feeling of discomfort or nervousness, when we need to talk to new people or are the center of attention. It can make us feel awkward and unsure of how to behave or what to say.

Social anxiety is a more intense form of fear, where we may experience overwhelming nervousness and fear of being judged or rejected. When plagued by social anxiety, we might encounter physical symptoms such as a racing heart, sweaty palms, or trembling when speaking with others.

These feelings can make it challenging for us to engage in conversations and build meaningful relationships. By understanding and acknowledging these emotions, we can work on strategies to overcome them and improve our social confidence.

If you struggle with shyness or social anxiety, the strategies in the following sections can benefit you. However, if you experience severe, all-consuming social anxiety, we strongly recommend seeking help and support from a therapist or psychologist. Social anxiety can be self-reinforcing, and professional help may be necessary to break the cycle. Remember, it's okay to ask for assistance—it's an essential step toward finding relief and regaining control of your life.

# Identify Triggers and Patterns

Often, we're not fully aware of what exactly causes us stress, triggers our shyness, or sets off our social anxiety. The first step is to figure out what brings out these feelings. By becoming more conscious of the triggers, we can better understand and address the situations that make us anxious.

For some, any form of social interaction can be a challenge. This includes everyday conversations, small talk at social gatherings, or starting a conversation with a stranger. For others, more specific situations trigger anxiety, such as speaking in front of a large group, participating in work meetings, or being the center of attention at social events.

When we take the time to reflect on our feelings and experiences, we can begin to identify patterns in our anxiety.

Identifying triggers and patterns is an exercise that can help you understand what causes discomfort or anxiety in social situations.

Observe your thoughts and reactions in different situations to start identifying what triggers your discomfort or concern. Consider what typically goes through your mind when you feel uneasy in social settings. It might be worried about how others perceive you or thoughts about being judged. Consider which types of conversations or interactions often make you nervous—are you uncomfortable when sharing personal experiences or when asked to express your opinion?

You can also ask yourself questions like: *"What am I thinking about when I feel anxious?"* or *"Which conversation topics make me the most nervous?"* These reflections can help you discover which thoughts and topics specifically trigger your anxiety. For example, if you often feel nervous when discussing personal matters, this might reveal that this is a significant trigger for you. Another example might be noticing that you feel anxious when expressing your opinion in a discussion, which could indicate a fear of being misunderstood or judged.

Consider questions such as: *"When was the last time I felt overwhelmed in a conversation?"* and *"What types of conversations do I often avoid?"* By being mindful of your behavior and choices, you can spot patterns that show which situations you find most challenging.

Identifying your triggers and patterns may feel challenging, but remember that each time you reflect on your thoughts and reactions, you're taking an essential step toward greater confidence in social situations. The more you practice, the easier it will become to recognize and manage the things that concern you. Be patient, and remember that every small effort brings you closer to your goal of feeling more comfortable and confident in conversations with others.

## Gradual Exposure

Once we become aware of what triggers explicitly our anxiety, gradual exposure can be an incredibly effective method for overcoming these challenges and building greater confidence in social settings. This method involves slowly exposing ourselves to the situations that cause us stress but in a controlled and manageable way.

A practical approach to gradual exposure is to start with small, achievable goals and progressively increase the level of challenge. If we struggle with shyness, we might begin with simple interactions, such as saying *"hi"* to neighbors or colleagues in the morning. As we become more comfortable with these small actions, we can try asking a stranger for the time or starting brief conversations, like asking how their weekend was.

Once we feel more at ease with these small interactions, we can gradually move on to more extended conversations or attend smaller social gatherings. For example, we could start by attending a small group event, where we know most participants, and then slowly challenge ourselves by attending more significant events or social gatherings with more unfamiliar faces. By gradually exposing ourselves to more challenging situations, we can steadily build our confidence and ability to manage social interactions.

Alternatively, if we feel anxious about shopping in a busy store, we could begin by visiting the store early in the morning, when there are fewer people. As we become more comfortable, we can gradually increase the challenge by shopping at busier times, until we feel more at ease. This step-by-step approach allows us to confront our anxiety in a way that doesn't feel overwhelming.

Gradual exposure helps us build confidence and reinforces the idea that we are more capable of handling social interactions, than we may have believed. Every time we complete a successful interaction, no matter how small, it strengthens our belief in our abilities and reduces our anxiety. We can achieve greater control and confidence in social situations by taking small steps and progressively increasing our exposure.

## GRADUAL EXPOSURE

Gradual exposure is a method that can help us build confidence and comfort in social situations. To get the most out of this exercise, we recommend using your journal to write down your goals and milestones.

Start by identifying your overall goal—perhaps you want to feel more confident in social settings or be able to speak freely in front of a group. Then, break this goal into smaller, more manageable steps you feel comfortable tackling. These smaller goals should be specific and realistic, such as greeting a colleague each morning or starting a brief conversation with a neighbor. By writing down these goals and milestones, you can track your progress and celebrate the small victories, motivating you to continue your journey toward feeling more comfortable with others and forming meaningful relationships.

Repetition is critical; the more you practice, the more natural your interactions will feel. Remember, the fear of starting conversations can be overcome. With the proper techniques and some practice, you can turn your anxiety into skill, making each interaction an opportunity for growth and connection.

## Building Confidence Through Visualization

Another effective strategy for tackling shyness and social anxiety is visualization. Our brain can create realities that feel just as real as our world. When we visualize successful conversations, we create mental images that boost our confidence and ability to communicate clearly and effectively.

Practicing visualization, we imagine detailed scenarios where we handle social situations with confidence and calm. One of the benefits of visualization is that it can reduce our anxiety and nervousness.

When we repeatedly picture ourselves managing social situations successfully, our brain starts to believe that we can do it in real life. For example, if we often feel nervous when speaking in large groups, we can visualize ourselves standing in front of an audience, speaking calmly and confidently. The more we practice this visualization, our confidence will grow, and our anxiety will diminish.

For instance, we can imagine ourselves conversing with a colleague where we speak clearly and confidently, or we can visualize giving a presentation that impresses the audience with our eloquence. Creating these mental images prepares our brain and body to respond positively in real situations.

Another advantage of visualization is that it can be done anywhere, anytime. We can take a few minutes daily to close our eyes and imagine ourselves in successful conversations and social interactions. This can be especially helpful before a challenging situation, such as a meeting or social event. By taking the time to visualize, we can calm our minds and mentally prepare ourselves to face the problem confidently.

## BUILDING CONFIDENCE THROUGH VISUALIZATION

Mental imagery training is a powerful method for mentally preparing ourselves for challenging situations.

Finding a quiet and safe place to relax without distractions is essential to get the most out of your mental images. Sit comfortably, close your eyes, and take a few deep breaths to calm your mind and body.

Imagine entering a room where you will give a presentation or participate in a conversation. Visualize yourself speaking clearly and distinctly, and notice how the people around you listen attentively and respond positively to your words. Picture yourself receiving approving nods and smiles and feel a sense of calm and security spreading through your body.

You can also imagine giving a presentation in front of your colleagues. Visualize yourself standing before your colleagues with good posture, taking calm breaths, and beginning to speak with a clear and confident voice. Picture your colleagues nodding and looking interested while taking notes. You continue to communicate clearly and distinctly throughout your presentation, and you finish with a smile as you receive approving praise and applause.

You can also imagine having a meaningful conversation with a friend about something bothering you. Visualize sitting together with your friend in a comfortable place. Picture yourself speaking clearly and calmly about your feelings without becoming emotionally overwhelmed. Imagine your friend listening attentively and responding with understanding and empathy. You make eye contact and feel a sense of relief and understanding, making you more confident in your communication skills.

Practice regularly with the situations you want to work on, preferably daily. Remember to take time to feel the positive emotions that the visualization evokes. This will strengthen your belief in your abilities and help you transfer this confidence to real-life conversations.

## Breathing and Relaxation Techniques

When we want to manage physical symptoms like a racing heart, sweaty palms, trembling, tense muscles, and shortness of breath that can arise from insecurity or anxiety, we can use techniques such as deep breathing, controlled muscle relaxation, and visualization.

### Breathing

Deep breathing helps us manage symptoms by lowering our heart rate, allowing us to feel calmer and more focused on the conversation instead of our anxiety.

When we breathe deeply and slowly, we activate the parasympathetic nervous system, which calms us and restores balance. Deep breathing also signals the brain that we are in a safe situation, reducing the production of stress hormones.

Deep breathing also enhances our ability to focus and be present in the moment. When stressed, we tend to breathe quickly and shallowly, which can intensify feelings of panic. By consciously breathing deeply, we can lower our heart rate and create a sense of calm. This allows us to concentrate better on the conversation and be more aware of what's happening around us.

Another benefit of deep breathing is that it's a simple technique we can use anywhere. Whether at work, at home, or on public transport, we can take a moment to breathe deeply and center ourselves. Its ease of use makes it simple to integrate into our daily routine, providing a practical tool to manage stress and anxiety.

## BREATHING

Breathing exercises are an effective technique for managing stressful situations. To use this technique in moments of pressure, start practicing deep breathing as part of your daily routine. Aim to practice deep breathing for at least five minutes daily for the best results.

You can practice this technique in the morning, before bed, or ahead of situations that usually make you nervous. Consider using a breathing app to help you keep track of time and pace.

Find a quiet place to sit comfortably or lie down without

being disturbed. Place one hand on your stomach and the other on your chest. This will help you feel how deeply you are breathing. Slowly inhale through your nose for four seconds, feeling your stomach expand under your hand. Hold your breath for four seconds, then slowly exhale through your mouth for six seconds, feeling your stomach fall. Repeat this cycle five to ten times or until you feel calmer and more relaxed.

Remember, breathing exercises require patience and repetition, and it's completely normal if it doesn't feel natural at first. Over time, you'll find that you become better at calming yourself in stressful situations.

## Controlled Muscle Relaxation

Controlled muscle relaxation is an exercise that can reduce physical tension and is especially useful in stressful situations where we feel tense. This technique helps us become more aware of how our body responds to stress. By consciously tensing and relaxing different muscle groups, we learn to recognize and release tension we might not have been aware of.

When we regularly practice controlled muscle relaxation, it will strengthen our ability to manage stress more effectively. In challenging situations, this technique helps calm our nervous system, reducing feelings of pressure. Additionally, muscle relaxation positively affects our mental well-being, as a relaxed body often leads to a calmer mind, making it easier to think clearly and make sound decisions.

One of the significant advantages of this exercise is its simplicity and accessibility as it requires no special equipment.

## CONTROLLED MUSCLE RELAXATION

Controlled muscle relaxation is an effective way to reduce stress and bring calm to the body. Start by finding a quiet and comfortable place to sit or lie down without interruptions. You could play some calming music or use a guided meditation to help you get into the right frame of mind.

As you work through each muscle group, it is essential to breathe deeply and steadily. Inhale through your nose as you tense your muscles, and exhale slowly through your mouth as you relax.

When you're ready, begin with your feet. Curl your toes to tense the muscles in your feet and hold the tension for about five seconds.

Pay attention to the feeling of tightness, then release the tension and relax for ten seconds, focusing on the sensation of relaxation spreading through your feet. Repeat this process a few times until you feel comfortable with the exercise.

Next, move to your calves and thighs. Tighten the muscles in your calves by pointing your toes toward you and holding the tension for five seconds. Release and relax for ten seconds. Then, tense the muscles in your thighs by pressing your knees together, holding, and following the same relaxation process.

Move up to your abdomen. Tighten your abdominal muscles by pulling your belly button toward your spine and holding for five seconds. Release the tension and feel the relaxation spread.

Continue to your upper body by tensing your chest and back muscles. Pull your shoulder blades together and hold for five seconds before relaxing.

Now, focus on your arms. Tighten the muscles in your upper arms by bending your elbows and holding the tension for five seconds. Release and feel the relaxation in your arms.

Next, move to your hands. Make fists and tighten the muscles for five seconds, then slowly open your hands and relax them.

Finally, focus on your face. Tense the muscles by furrowing your brows, squeezing your eyes shut, and clenching your jaw for five seconds. Release the tension, allowing the muscles in your face to relax.

Systematically completing this exercise, you will learn to recognize the difference between tense and relaxed muscles.

This can help you reduce physical tension and achieve a more profound sense of calm and well-being in your daily life.

## Visualization

Visualization is another effective exercise. This method uses our imagination to picture a calm and peaceful place. This method helps reduce stress and create a sense of calm and balance, no matter where we are.

Imagine a safe and relaxing place, such as a quiet beach, a lush forest, or a mountain landscape. We can let go of everyday worries and find mental peace. This mental focus can enhance our concentration and resilience, making it easier to handle stressful situations.

The visualization exercise can also trigger physical responses, such as lowering our heart rate and relaxing our muscles, which increases our sense of well-being. It can also improve the quality of our sleep by calming the mind before bed, making it easier to fall asleep and sleep deeply. Additionally, this exercise can boost our creative thinking, stimulate our imagination, and open up new perspectives and ideas.

One of the great benefits of the visualization exercise is its simplicity. It can be used, without special equipment or much time.

Visualizing calm and relaxation is an effective way to soothe the mind. Begin by finding a quiet place to sit or lie comfortably. Close your eyes and imagine a place that feels safe and relaxing, whether it's a beach, a forest, a mountain landscape, a garden, a quiet lake, or perhaps a cozy library. Visualize the details, such as the sounds, scents, and colors.

For example, imagine a cozy log cabin deep in the forest, where you are sitting in front of a crackling fireplace. You can hear the soothing sound of wood popping and cracking as the flames dance in the hearth.

The warm, golden glow from the fire casts soft shadows on the rough wooden walls, and you feel the warmth from the fireplace slowly spreading throughout the room, enveloping you in a comforting sense of safety and ease.

Outside, you can just make out the sound of soft snow falling while you sit wrapped in a soft blanket, holding a cup of hot cocoa in your hands, with the calming scent of burning wood filling the room, creating a deep sense of peace and serenity.

Alternatively, you might imagine standing on a mountaintop at sunset, where a cool breeze gently brushes against your face, and you breathe in the fresh, clean mountain air. The sky shifts from a deep orange to shades of purple and pink as the sun slowly sinks behind the snow-capped peaks.

You can hear the faint whisper of the wind moving through the tall pine trees below and perhaps catch the scent of pine and fresh snow in the air. The sun's last rays cast long shadows across the landscape, painting the mountains in golden and purple hues, while a feeling of peace and awe embraces you.

Another option could be picturing a calm lake at dawn, where the water's surface mirrors the sky's soft pastel hues as the first rays of sunlight slowly warm the landscape. You can feel the cool morning dew on the grass beneath your feet, hear the birds beginning their first songs, and perhaps smell the fresh, clean air mixed with a faint scent of forest and wildflowers. The water's surface is so still that it looks like glass, and every movement creates small, perfect ripples that disappear as quickly as they form.

Remember, visualization is a powerful personal exercise that you can shape to suit your needs and desires. Finding the images that bring you the most profound sense of peace may take some practice, but be patient with yourself in the process.

Each time you immerse yourself in these mental images, you strengthen your ability to find calm and focus, even in challenging situations.

## Strengthen Your Inner Voice

Another essential way to address our insecurities is by becoming aware of our inner dialogue. Our conversations with ourselves are crucial in how we perceive and respond to the world around us. Our inner voice can either be our best friend or our worst enemy. A negative inner voice can prevent us from using even the best communication techniques by creating doubt and uncertainty that undermine our confidence and hinder our ability to express ourselves clearly and confidently.

However, understanding how we talk to ourselves and learning to manage our inner dialogue can change how we handle challenges and positively impact our emotions. This not only improves our communication skills but also has a positive effect on our behavior in all areas of life.

A positive inner dialogue can boost our confidence and motivation, while a negative one can drag us into a spiral of doubt and insecurity.

How we talk to ourselves isn't just background noise—it profoundly influences how we view ourselves and react in daily life.

For example, if we face a challenge and think, *"I never do anything right,"* it affects our mood, self-esteem, and future actions. Another negative thought could be, *"I'm not good enough for this,"* which can cause us to avoid new challenges and limit our growth. On the other hand, if we think, *"How can I improve?"* or *"What can I learn from this?"* we're already on the path to communicating with ease and confidence, fostering deeper connections with others. This shift in mindset helps us embrace opportunities for growth and development.

To change our inner dialogue, we can use strategies like becoming aware of our thoughts and replacing negative ones with empowering statements. This positive approach can make a significant difference, personally and professionally, as it helps us better handle challenges and view potential setbacks as learning opportunities, ultimately increasing our confidence.

Transforming negative self-talk into positive affirmations is a powerful way to build confidence. To help you develop a more positive inner dialogue, you can practice some simple daily exercises that will strengthen your inner voice:

## Daily Affirmations

Start each day by saying positive affirmations out loud to yourself. These might include statements like, *"I am capable and competent," "I can handle any challenge,"* or *"I can create strong and meaningful relationships."* By repeating these affirmations, you train your brain to think positively about yourself.

Write down the affirmations that resonate most with you in your journal.

## Write Three Positive Things

Each evening, write down three positive things that happened during the day. These can be big or small events if they make you happy or proud. This exercise will help you focus on the positive and develop a habit of seeing the good in your daily life.

## Challenge Negative Thoughts

When you notice a negative thought, pause and ask yourself if that thought is true. Is there evidence to support it, or is it your insecurity speaking?

Try replacing negative thoughts with more realistic and positive alternatives. For example, if you think, *"I'm bad at talking to new people,"* you can replace it with, *"I can get better at talking to new people, and I'm taking small steps every day to improve.*" Or if you think, *"No one will listen to what I have to say,"* you can change it to, *"I have valuable things to share, and I will find the right times and ways to express myself."* By reframing your thoughts in this way, you can create a more positive and supportive inner dialogue.

Practicing these techniques in a safe environment can make a real difference. Remember the strategies we've discussed, like identifying your anxiety-triggers, using gradual exposure, applying visualization, and strengthening your inner voice.

Regularly practicing these techniques will become part of your routine, and you will find it easier to calm yourself, when you feel nervous.

# Chapter 2

# THE FOUNDATION OF EFFECTIVE COMMUNICATION

Imagine how your conversations would change if you truly understood what was being said—not just through words but also through everything left unsaid. In this chapter, we dive into how we can communicate with a more profound understanding.

We'll explore how to improve our listening skills through practical exercises and turn them into strengths in everyday interactions. By practicing active listening, where we show genuine attention and interest, we can begin to hear the words and become better at sensing the emotions behind them.

We'll also discover the significance of body language and eye contact—how they can reinforce or alter messages, and how we can use these tools to create deeper connections with the people we talk to. By learning to interpret and respond to subtle cues like facial expressions and posture, we'll be able to engage in conversations with greater empathy and understanding.

Throughout this chapter, we will improve our ability to express ourselves and become more attuned to picking up on and responding to the needs and feelings of others. It's about building better connections between people and fostering stronger, deeper, and more honest relationships. With these tools, we can communicate in a way that conveys information and creates meaning and connection.

## What Are Conversations?

Conversations are a big part of our everyday lives and serve various purposes. They help us build deeper connections, achieve our goals, or pass the time. To understand what we want to accomplish with our conversations, it's essential to consider the different objectives they can have.

### Building Deeper Connections

One of the most meaningful reasons to talk with others is to create and strengthen our relationships. Through conversations, we share our thoughts, feelings, and experiences, fostering a sense of closeness and understanding.

Engaging in deep and honest discussions allows us to build trust and intimacy with those we care about. This is especially important in close friendships, family relationships, and romantic partnerships, where conversations bridge hearts and minds.

### Achieving Our Goals

Another vital function of conversations is achieving specific goals or desires. This could involve completing a task, negotiating a deal, or reaching a decision. Effective communication is crucial in these situations, as it consists of presenting our viewpoints clearly and persuasively while listening to and respecting the other person's perspectives.

## Passing the Time

Conversations also serve the simple purpose of passing time. Small talk or casual conversations help break the silence and create a comfortable atmosphere, making social situations less awkward. This often happens in everyday situations, like waiting in line at the grocery store, grabbing coffee at a café, or sharing an elevator with a colleague.

## Sharing Knowledge and Learning

Conversations are also a fundamental way to share knowledge and learn. They allow us to exchange information, learn new things, and gain fresh perspectives. This often happens in educational settings, at work, or when seeking advice from a friend or mentor.

Conversations are unavoidable in daily life and are much more than just the exchange of words. By being mindful of what we want to achieve in our discussions, we can improve our communication skills and build stronger relationships. Whether we're looking to deepen connections, accomplish a task, or simply pass the time, mastering the various aspects of conversation helps us get the most out of every interaction.

In the next section, we will examine active listening, one of the most effective ways to ensure our conversations lead to genuine understanding and connection.

## Active Listening: The Key to Effective Communication

Active listening isn't just an important skill; it's the foundation of all effective communication. When we listen actively, we do more than just hear the words—we engage in the conversation in a way that creates a deeper connection and fosters mutual respect and understanding. Active listening is about understanding the words, emotions, and intentions behind them.

This is crucial because if we don't truly hear what the other person is saying, it becomes challenging to ask relevant questions, offer thoughtful responses, or carry the conversation forward meaningfully.

We ensure we've understood the message correctly by summarizing what the other person has said before sharing our thoughts. It's important not to repeat the words like a parrot, but to truly listen and show that we understand the content and the emotion behind what's being said. This also demonstrates that we respect the other person's perspective, creating a solid foundation for the rest of the conversation. For example, if a friend talks about a challenging situation at work, we could summarize by saying, *"So, if I understand correctly, you're feeling overwhelmed by the workload lately?"* This confirms that we've heard and understood their concerns and allows us to ask follow-up questions to deepen the conversation.

In another scenario, if a friend is sharing frustrations about a misunderstanding with another friend, we might summarize by saying, *"What I'm hearing is that you feel misunderstood and vulnerable in this situation?"* This shows that we've been paying close attention and allows our friend to elaborate on their feelings, leading to a more supportive and meaningful dialogue.

In family life, active listening is also vital in building strong relationships. If a child expresses frustration with their homework, we could summarize by saying, *"So, you're finding the math assignments difficult, and it's making you frustrated?"* This understanding forms the basis for offering support or asking the right questions to help the child move forward.

When we master active listening, we create more effective communication and lay the groundwork for the rest of the conversation. By listening attentively, we can ask questions that truly matter and respond in a way that strengthens the connection between us and the person we're speaking with. Whether in a personal, professional, or family context, active listening is the key to deeper understanding and stronger relationships.

## ACTIVE LISTENING: THE KEY TO EFFECTIVE COMMUNICATION

Practicing active listening can be a powerful way to improve your communication skills. The next time you're conversing, summarize what you hear before sharing your thoughts.

This practice serves two purposes: it helps you genuinely listen to the speaker and shows the person that their words are valuable to you.

For example, if a colleague explains a complex project where there is too little time to complete it, you could summarize by saying, *"So, if I understand correctly, your main concern is the tight deadline."* This shows that you've grasped their point without immediately offering a solution.

Or if your friend is telling you about a challenging situation at home, you might say, *"It sounds like this has been tough for you."* This demonstrates empathy and allows your friend to continue sharing their feelings.

If a family member expresses concern about something, you could say, *"So, you're worried about how this will affect our plans."* This shows that you're taking their concerns seriously and allowing them to elaborate on their thoughts.

Keep practicing this technique to strengthen your listening ability and enhance your communication in personal and professional relationships.

## Nonverbal Cues

Our communication consists of verbal and nonverbal cues crucial in sharing information and emotions. While verbal cues involve the words we choose, nonverbal cues involve our body language, facial expressions, tone of voice, and gestures.

It might seem evident that words play the most significant role, but nonverbal cues often emphasize and reinforce our messages. Understanding nonverbal signals can improve our ability to engage with others and foster honest, meaningful conversations. These cues help us capture emotions and intentions that words alone might not express, allowing us to respond more thoughtfully and support each other better in interactions.

Nonverbal cues are vital in supporting our verbal messages. When our body language, facial expressions, and tone of voice align with what we're saying, it strengthens and clarifies our message. For example, smiling and making eye contact while saying something positive makes us appear more sincere and engaged. This can make the conversation more effective and help build trust and understanding.

However, if our nonverbal cues don't match our words, it can create confusion and mistrust. For instance, if we say *"I'm fine"* with a frown and crossed arms, the listener will likely doubt our sincerity and feel uncertain about what we mean. This mismatch can lead to misunderstandings and disrupt the flow of conversation, so we must be mindful of our verbal and nonverbal cues. In other words, we must ensure our consistent signals convey a clear and cohesive message.

Understanding and interpreting others' nonverbal cues is just as important as being aware of ourselves. It's about observing the alignment between what a person says, and what their body language shows us.

When we become attuned to nonverbal cues in conversations, we can use our observations to create more meaningful and profound dialogue. For example, if we notice someone saying they're okay but nervously fidgeting with their hands or shifting their weight from foot to foot, it might indicate they're not feeling completely comfortable. In this case, we could say, *"I notice you seem a bit restless. Is there something on your mind we could talk about?"* By showing that we're paying attention to these subtle signals, we create a safe space for the other person to share what's happening, strengthening the conversation and the relationship.

We can also use our observations to adjust our communication. If we notice a colleague crossing their arms and avoiding eye contact during a discussion, it might signal that they feel unsure or defensive. In this situation, we could open our posture by uncrossing our arms, leaning forward slightly, and speaking softer. We might say, *"I'd like to hear your thoughts—what do you think about what we're discussing?"* This can help create a more comfortable and open conversation.

Another example could be noticing that a friend seems nervous during a conversation, perhaps shifting their weight or avoiding eye contact. In this case, we can help create a calmer atmosphere by lowering our voices, maintaining a relaxed posture, and offering a friendly smile. We might say, *"It seems like something is on your mind. Should we take a break and talk about it?"* This can help ease their anxiety and open up a more honest dialogue.

Here's an overview of different nonverbal cues and how we can use them to improve our communication and, in turn, build deeper relationships.

## The Power of Vocal Tone

Although we might think that vocal tone is part of verbal communication, it is part of nonverbal communication. Vocal tone refers to how we use our voice to convey emotions and intentions, making it a crucial aspect of nonverbal cues.

Our pitch, volume, speed, and pauses can significantly change the meaning of our words. For instance, a phrase like *"I'm happy to see you"* can have entirely different meanings depending on how it's said. If delivered with a warm and enthusiastic tone, it expresses genuine happiness. But if spoken with a monotone or flat voice, it may come across as sarcastic or indifferent.

By fine-tuning our tone, pace, volume, and the strategic use of pauses, we can enhance our ability to convey our message most engagingly and persuasively.

## The Importance of Pace in Communication

The pace, or speed at which we speak, is a critical factor in communication because it affects how listeners receive and interpret our messages. Babbling can signal enthusiasm, engagement, or a sense of urgency to get information across quickly. However, this fast pace can also overwhelm the listener, especially if sustained over a long period, making it difficult for them to keep up or absorb what's being said. For this reason, it can be helpful to adjust the pace by slowing down when the listener needs time to reflect on or process the information.

On the other hand, speaking too slowly can give the impression that we need to be more confident or even uninterested in the topic. A languid pace can cause the conversation to lose momentum, which may lead the listener to lose interest. It can create the sense that the conversation is dragging, causing the message to lose its impact.

Finding a balance in our pace is essential, matching the tempo to the context and the people we speak with. Varying our pace throughout the conversation can keep listeners more engaged. For instance, we speed up our speech when expressing excitement or making a critical point, then slow down to allow an essential piece of information to sink in. This balanced tempo creates a rhythm in our speech that makes our communication more dynamic and effective while also helping to maintain the listener's attention and understanding.

## The Role of Volume in Communication

We should be mindful of our volume to ensure it matches the content of our message. Speaking loudly can project confidence and draw attention in a large room. For example, a powerful voice can help keep everyone engaged when presenting a project to a team. Conversely, speaking softly can draw people closer to an intimate conversation. A gentle voice can create a sense of closeness and confidentiality when sharing something personal with a friend.

## The Effect of Pauses in Communication

Pauses are a powerful tool that can enhance our communication, whether speaking to one person, a small group, or a larger audience. Pausing allows listeners time to absorb our words and reflect on what has been said. We can use pauses to emphasize our points and improve the rhythm and flow of our speech.

A well-placed pause after a vital statement can highlight its significance and impact the audience more deeply. Similarly, pausing before delivering crucial information can build anticipation and make the upcoming message more impactful.

## The Importance of Facial Expressions in Communiction

Our facial expressions act like a billboard, reflecting our emotions even before we say the first word. Examples include a smile that conveys happiness or friendliness, furrowed brows that signal confusion or concern, and raised eyebrows that often indicate surprise or interest. Pursed lips can show anger or frustration, while a nod indicates agreement or understanding. These expressions reveal our emotions and attitudes and play a crucial role in how others receive and understand our message.

When our facial expressions align with our words, we appear more genuine and credible, significantly strengthening our message. For example, smiling sincerely when offering praise or looking serious when discussing something important makes us seem more sincere to our listeners. On the other hand, a mismatch between our facial expression and what we're saying—like a smile while delivering bad news—can create confusion and undermine our credibility. Therefore, we must be aware of our facial expressions and ensure they align with our words to communicate clearly and effectively.

## The Power of Eye Contact

Eye contact is a vital aspect of body language that signals interest, confidence, and sincerity. In many cultures, maintaining eye contact is seen as a sign of attentiveness and respect. However, balance is critical. Avoiding eye contact can come across as disinterest or dishonesty, while too much eye contact can feel intrusive. To find a natural balance, we must consider the situation, the people we are talking to, and their comfort levels. In professional settings, such as a business meeting, maintaining eye contact shows attentiveness and interest, signaling that we are engaged and taking the conversation seriously. In more casual social situations, like conversations with friends or family, we can adjust eye contact to create a comfortable and relaxed atmosphere. This might mean breaking eye contact occasionally to avoid appearing too intense or imposing.

## The Role of Posture in Communication

Our posture often communicates more than we realize and can reveal much about our attitude and emotional state. An open posture—uncrossed arms, a straight back, and a relaxed stance—signals openness, approachability, and a willingness to engage. For instance, standing with feet slightly apart, shoulders back, and arms relaxed at our sides projects confidence and availability. This can make the other person feel more at ease and willing to open up during the conversation.

Conversely, a closed posture, such as crossed arms or tense muscles, may indicate defensiveness, discomfort, or disinterest. For example, sitting in a meeting with arms crossed and shoulders hunched might give the impression that we're not open to others' viewpoints or are uninterested in the conversation.

Our posture dramatically influences how others perceive us and our message. By being mindful of our body language, we can choose to stand or sit in ways that support the type of communication we want. For example, if we project confidence and openness during a presentation, we can stand with feet firmly planted, shoulders back, and hands visibly relaxed at our sides.

This signals that we are confident in our message and open to dialogue, which can enhance how the audience perceives both us and our presentation.

## Gestures and Communication

Gestures include movements with our hands, arms, and heads to support and reinforce our spoken words. They are essential to body language and can help clarify and make our message more engaging.

Examples of gestures include nodding to show agreement or understanding, pointing to emphasize something specific, using hands to illustrate the size or shape of something, waving to attract attention or signal hello or goodbye, and clapping hands to emphasize a key point or express excitement. These movements help bring our words to life and make our communication more dynamic and easier to understand.

However, gestures should be used thoughtfully, like all forms of body language. Excessive gesturing can distract from our message and make us appear restless or nervous. On the other hand, too little movement can make us seem stiff or disengaged. It's essential to find a balance where our gestures feel natural and appropriate to what we're saying.

## Effective Mirroring in Communication

Mirroring is a powerful technique in body language that helps us build mutual understanding and establish a sense of connection. When we communicate, we subtly mimic the other person's body language. If they lean forward, we can do the same; if they gesture with their hands, we can mirror similar movements.

This should be done discreetly, as obvious mirroring can be perceived as mockery. When used thoughtfully, mirroring can create a sense of harmony, making the conversation flow more smoothly.

## NONVERBAL SIGNALS

It's essential to put theory into practice to improve your communication skills. By practicing specific techniques, you can start using them in your daily conversations and become more aware of how you communicate.

Set aside time each day to work on different aspects of vocal tone, pace, volume, pauses, facial expressions, eye contact, posture, gestures, and mirroring.

Start with a vocal tone by choosing a simple sentence like *"I'm happy to see you"* and experiment with different pitches and volumes, while saying it aloud in front of a mirror.

Notice how changes in your voice affect your perception of the sentence. Once you feel comfortable, try incorporating varied vocal tones into your conversations to adapt your message to different situations.

For pace, try reading aloud from a book or article, consciously varying the speed at which you speak. Read a passage quickly and then slowly, noting how the pace affects your understanding and delivery. Apply this awareness to conversations by speaking more slowly to emphasize key points and faster when expressing excitement or enthusiasm.

Volume is another crucial factor in effective communication. Practice adjusting your vocal volume by reading a text aloud and gradually increasing or decreasing the loudness. When speaking with others, use this technique to ensure your voice is clear and audible without being overwhelming or subdued.

To work on the impact of pauses, take a short passage and practice inserting pauses after keywords or meaningful sentences. This helps to give your words more weight and allows the listener time to absorb the information. For example, after saying, *"This is important,"* pause to emphasize what follows. Or, if you say, *"We need to make a decision,"* pause after *"decision"* to highlight the significance of the choice. Pausing after these keywords creates a more significant impact on your communication.

In conversations, consciously incorporate pauses before important statements to create anticipation or underscore a point. This gives your words more weight and makes it easier for your conversation partner to understand and appreciate them.

Eye contact is a powerful tool in any conversation. Practice maintaining eye contact with your reflection in the mirror as you speak. Notice how it feels to hold eye contact for varying lengths of time. Try applying this in your conversations by maintaining eye contact, while adjusting it based on the situation to create a sense of connection without sounding too intense.

You can also practice posture and gestures by standing in front of a mirror and intentionally changing your stance and movements. Try standing straight back and shoulders relaxed while speaking, and observe how it affects your confidence.

Incorporate different hand gestures to support your words, and be mindful of how it feels to use gestures actively in your communication.

Mirroring is a technique you can practice by observing others during conversations. Notice their posture, movements, and vocal tone, and try to mirror these elements subtly. After the discussion, reflect on how the mirroring affected your dynamic and connection.

These exercises can become part of your daily routine, gradually increasing your awareness of the various aspects of your communication.

The more you practice, the more natural it will feel and the easier it will be to apply these techniques in everyday conversations. Remember, communication is a skill that improves over time, and each conversation is an opportunity to refine and enhance your abilities.

Understanding and using verbal and nonverbal signals in your communication gives you a solid foundation for creating more meaningful and effective conversations. This awareness of your own and others' body language, vocal tone, and facial expressions puts you in a stronger position to engage with others authentically and empathetically.

Now that you have the essential tools to improve your communication, the next step is to learn how to keep conversations going and deepen them. Starting a conversation is vital, but sustaining it and creating more profound, meaningful dialogues is just as crucial. In the next chapter, we'll explore strategies and techniques to help you build on conversations, ask the right questions, and navigate discussions to ensure they remain engaging and productive.

Chapter 3:

# CONVERSATION TECHNIQUES

Once we've learned how to start a conversation, the next step is to keep it going and make it more interesting. It's not just about talking but also about listening, asking the right questions, and knowing when to dive deeper or keep things light. This chapter will explore techniques that help us navigate conversations naturally and empathetically, allowing us to build stronger, more meaningful relationships.

## The Communication Ladder: A Practical Guide to Starting and Building Conversations

Imagine that every conversation is like a ladder, with each rung representing a new level of depth and understanding. The ladder serves as both a guide and inspiration, helping us pace the conversation in a way that feels right for us and the person we're talking to.

For example, we might begin by discussing something neutral and noncommittal. As trust and comfort grow, we can take the conversation to a higher level where we share personal experiences or feelings.

If, at any point, the conversation feels too intense or uncomfortable, we can always choose to step back down the ladder to a more comfortable level. This ensures the conversation remains safe and positive without feeling pressured to share more than we're ready to. This method not only provides a structured approach to building conversations but also offers the flexibility to adapt to the natural flow of the dialogue. We learn to be mindful of our boundaries and those of the other person, and we gain the tools to navigate conversations to foster more robust and meaningful relationships.

## The First Step: Making a Good First Impression

The communication ladder's first step is creating a positive first impression. Research shows that we often form impressions of each other within the first few minutes of a meeting, influencing how our conversations unfold. That's why making a good first impression is crucial.

As discussed earlier, nonverbal signals play a central role in this process. Our body language, appearance, and behavior can quickly signal who we are and what we stand for. Our clothing and posture should reflect that we take the situation seriously, if we're at a formal event. We can choose attire and behavior that reflect our style and comfort in more casual settings.

Our body language should project confidence and openness. Standing tall, maintaining eye contact, and smiling all send positive signals, contributing to a welcoming atmosphere. We can still show engagement even when sitting straight with our feet flat on the ground and using our hands naturally while speaking. We should avoid crossing our arms, which can signal resistance. When listening, we can lean slightly forward and use consistent eye contact and nodding to show that we are attentive and engaged.

## The Second Step: The Initial Conversation

The second step on the ladder is choosing conversation topics that create a relaxed and pleasant atmosphere. Light conversation topics are easy to discuss and don't require deep personal insight. These topics help break the ice and make finding common ground easier without feeling pressured to share anything too personal.

Light conversation topics might include questions like, *"How's your day been?"* or *"Do you have any exciting plans for the weekend?"* These questions aren't intrusive and allow others to share something about themselves without feeling exposed. Other good examples include talking about the weather, the latest movie or TV show they've watched, or asking about their favorite restaurant in the area.

In more formal settings, such as a business meeting, we might start with something like, *"Thank you for meeting with me. I'm looking forward to discussing our project."* This sets a professional tone and shows we're ready to engage in the conversation.

In social gatherings like dinners or coffee outings, we can begin with a more personal and friendly tone, such as, *"Which neighborhood do you live in?"* or *"What brought you here tonight?"* These are easy questions to answer and can open the door to more personal conversations.

Using light conversation topics in the early stages of a discussion ensures that the communication stays comfortable. Once a relaxed atmosphere is established, we can explore more personal and in-depth issues if it feels natural for both of us. This approach helps guide the conversation in a way that respects the other person's comfort zone.

## The Third Step: Expanding the Conversation

Once we've taken the first steps on the communication ladder and established a good connection, we can begin exploring deeper topics using open and insightful questions. These questions are vital to keeping the conversation flowing and fostering a more substantial understanding between us and the person we speak with.

Open-ended questions are particularly effective because they invite others to share more about themselves. Unlike closed questions, which can often be answered with a simple *"yes"* or *"no,"* open-ended questions require more detailed responses, adding depth to the conversation.

To make this easier, we can think of open questions as those that start with words like *"what," "how," "why," "who," "where,"* or *"when."* These questions encourage explanations, descriptions, or personal reflections, leading to a more engaged dialogue.

For example, instead of asking, *"Did you have a good weekend?"*—which can be answered briefly—we might ask, *"What did you do over the weekend?"* This opens the conversation, allowing the other person to share their experiences and thoughts. Similarly, instead of asking, *"Do you like your job?"* we could ask, *"What made you choose your current job?"* This prompts a discussion about the person's motivations and career choices, providing deeper insight into their life.

We show genuine interest in the other person's perspective and experiences by using open-ended questions. This can lead to conversations that aren't just surface-level but build a stronger connection between us. For instance, if a friend has just returned from a vacation, we might ask, *"What was the highlight of your trip?"* rather than simply asking, *"Was it a good trip?"* This invites them to share more detailed and meaningful experiences, making the conversation more engaging.

Once we've used open and insightful questions to deepen the conversation, we can consider moving on to even deeper topics on the next ladder rung.

## The Fourth and Final Step: In-Depth Conversations

As the conversation flows, we can start asking follow-up questions, tailoring our questions based on what we hear. This shows that we are listening and genuinely interested in understanding more. The final step on the ladder is about creating a deeper, more meaningful dialogue where we genuinely connect with the other person personally.

To understand follow-up questions, consider them a natural extension of the conversation. They build on something the other person has already said and are designed to dig deeper into the topic, showing that we are fully engaged. Follow-up questions often begin with phrases like *"Can you tell me more,"* *"How,"* or *"What happened next?"*

These encourage the other person to provide more detailed or insightful answers. Instead of simply accepting a response and moving on, follow-up questions help us delve further into the content, often resulting in more nuanced and enriching discussions.

For example, if a friend says, *"I spent the weekend catching up with some old school friends,"* a follow-up question could be, *"That sounds like a great weekend! How was it seeing them again after so long? What made your time together special?"*

This not only shows that we're interested in their experience, but it also values the relationships that matter to them. By asking this way, we invite our friend to share more about their emotions and reflections on the experience.

Or, if a family member says, *"I've been spending a lot of time working on the garden to make it look nice,"* a follow-up question might be, *"That must have taken a lot of effort! Which part of the garden are you most proud of? How does it feel to see the finished result?"* This shows that we recognize their hard work and are curious about their sense of accomplishment. By asking in this manner, we create a conversation that allows the family members to share more about their passion and commitment.

Follow-up questions act as the engine of a conversation, keeping it going and steering it in a direction where both participants can get more out of the dialogue. They create a dynamic where the other person feels valued and understood, because we actively show interest in what they say. This can lead to more prosperous, more meaningful conversations that help build stronger relationships.

As we become more skilled at asking follow-up questions, we also become better at creating connections beyond the surface, allowing us to learn more about the people we're talking with. This technique is valuable in personal relationships and professional conversations, where deeper understanding can be crucial to success.

## Step Back Down the Ladder: Returning to Lighter Topics

Even with the best intentions, a deep conversation can sometimes become uncomfortable or make us feel like a boundary is being approached. In these moments, stepping back without making the conversation awkward is essential. The communication ladder makes it easy to shift from deep topics to lighter ones, helping maintain a pleasant atmosphere. This is especially crucial when the conversation veers into complex or sensitive subjects, such as personal loss, conflicts, or other challenging experiences.

When the conversation becomes too heavy, we can gently shift to a lighter topic to create a more comfortable mood. We might say, *"I can see this has been hard for you. Maybe we could talk about something that gives you hope. Have you experienced anything recently that made you smile?"* This shows empathy and concern for their well-being. Another way to lighten the tone is to mention something current and informal, such as, *"I saw you posted some pictures from your last trip. How was it?"* This steers the conversation toward something positive and engaging while respecting their feelings.

If the conversation has previously touched on complex topics, like a friend's recent loss or a colleague's work stress, it can be helpful to shift focus to lighter subjects to give them a break from heavy thoughts. For example, *"It sounds like you've been dealing with a lot. What do you do to relax and find some peace?"* This gives them a chance to share something more uplifting and positive.

Being able to change the topic naturally helps maintain a smooth conversation where both people feel comfortable and engaged. It ensures the conversation remains positive and stress-free, showing that we're attentive to the other person's comfort level. This makes maintaining a good mood and positive interactions easier, which is essential for creating and maintaining solid relationships.

## Ending the Conversation

Ending a conversation well is just as important as starting it right. Depending on the depth of the discussion and the topic, we can conclude the conversation at any point on the communication ladder.

If we're in the early steps, where the conversation is still light and casual, we can end it with a simple and polite remark. For example, *"It was nice talking with you. Let's enjoy the rest of the party."* This shows that we appreciate the conversation but are ready to move on.

When the conversation has become more profound but not too personal, we can use more specific closing statements. For instance, *"I've enjoyed hearing about your project. Let's catch up on it another time."* This signals that we're interested in continuing the conversation in the future.

If the conversation has reached a personal and profound level, ending it with empathy and respect is essential. We could say, *"I really appreciate you sharing that with me. I hope we can continue this conversation soon."* This shows that we respect their openness and are interested in continuing the dialogue.

Throughout the conversation, we should also be aware of signs that it's coming to a natural end. These might include frequent glances at the clock, pauses in the conversation, or the other person physically pulling back. In more intense discussions, body language like crossed arms, frustration, or a defensive tone may signal that it's time to wrap things up.

When we decide it's time to end the conversation, it's essential to do so in a positive way. Use polite yet precise closing phrases. For example, at a networking event, we might say, *"It's been great learning about your work. Let's exchange contact information so we can continue this conversation later."* This signals that we're ending the conversation but are interested in future interactions. In casual settings, we could say, *"I don't want to keep you any longer, but let's catch up again soon!"* Being transparent is essential to avoid any awkwardness.

Sometimes, suggesting a follow-up is helpful, especially if the conversation is essential or requires further discussion. For example, *"I have another appointment soon, but this is important. Can we schedule a call early next week to continue?"* This shows that we respect our time and theirs and are committed to continuing the dialogue.

If we're dealing with a persistent conversation partner who doesn't pick up on our signals, we'll need to be direct but still polite. We could say, *"I've really enjoyed our conversation and appreciate your insights. I must go now, but let's continue this again."* If the person continues talking, we may need to reinforce our words with body language, such as standing up or moving toward the exit, to underline that we are concluding the conversation.

Ending a conversation well ensures we leave a positive impression and maintain good relationships. Whether it's a casual chat or an intense debate, how we close the conversation shapes our personal and professional lives. Following the communication ladder, we can smoothly navigate conversations from start to finish, creating more profound and meaningful interactions.

# THE COMMUNICATION LADDER

The communication ladder's step-by-step approach helps us manage conversations more effectively. It starts with light topics and moves toward more profound, meaningful discussions.

Try the following exercises to practice this method and improve your conversational skills. These will help you apply the different stages of a conversation, allowing you to practice making good first impressions, expanding conversations, navigating deeper discussions, and stepping back to lighter topics when necessary.

<u>Exercise 1:</u>
**Create a Strong First Impression**
Begin by engaging in everyday conversations, focusing on the first few moments. Present yourself confidently by offering a firm handshake, maintaining eye contact, and giving a warm smile. After the conversation, reflect on how it went:

How did you feel? What body language did you use? What worked well, and what could you improve? Repeat this exercise in various settings, and observe how your first impressions evolve.

<u>Exercise 2:</u>

**Mastering the Initial Conversation**

This exercise aims to help you become more comfortable and confident when starting conversations with light, informal topics. It will give you a solid foundation for establishing connections and building trust.

Start by thinking about a few conversation topics that you feel comfortable discussing. These could include weekend plans, movies, books, travel, or current events. Write down a list of 3-5 topics you can quickly bring up in different situations.

Create at least one open-ended question for each topic on your list that invites a detailed response. For example, if you choose weekend plans, you could ask: *"Do you have any exciting plans for the weekend?"* or *"What do you enjoy doing in your free time?"*

If you choose travel as a topic, you could ask: *"If you could travel anywhere in the world right now, where would you go and why?"* or *"What's your most memorable travel experience, and what made it so special?"* These questions encourage your conversation partner to share personal experiences and dreams, opening up a conversation about cultures, destinations, and travel adventures.

The next time you're in a social setting—whether at work, a party, or a more informal gathering—try starting a conversation with one of your prepared topics and questions. Notice how the conversation develops and pay attention to the other person's reactions.

After the conversation, take a moment to reflect on how it went. Which topics worked best? Did you feel comfortable with your questions? Was there anything you could have done differently? Write down your thoughts so you can improve your approach for next time.

Use your reflection to adjust your approach if necessary. Try introducing new topics or questions in future conversations. Repeat this exercise regularly to build your confidence and ability to start and lead conversations easily.

This exercise will help you feel more comfortable using light conversation topics to create a natural and relaxed conversation start. Regularly practicing and reflecting on your experiences will strengthen your communication ability and form meaningful connections.

### Exercise 3:
### Explore Deeper Topics

To practice using open-ended questions and fostering deeper conversations, start by choosing a friend, colleague, or family member to practice with. This could be during a coffee break, a walk, or a casual chat at home.

Before the conversation, consider some open-ended

questions you'd like to ask. Focus on topics you know interest the other person or something they've mentioned recently. Open-ended questions can't be answered with a simple *"yes"* or *"no"*; they invite the other person to expand on their responses.

Begin the conversation with a general question, and when the opportunity arises, ask your open-ended questions. Remember to show genuine interest in the other person's answers and actively listen as they share their thoughts and experiences.

If they've mentioned a trip, you could ask, *"What was the most memorable part of your trip?"* or *"How did that experience impact you?"*

If they've talked about a project at work, you could ask, *"What has been the biggest challenge in the project you're working on?"* or *"What have you learned from that process?"*

If they've shared a personal experience, you might ask, *"How has that experience changed your perspective?"* or *"What did you feel when that happened?"*

Pay attention to how the conversation shifts when you use open-ended questions. Notice if the person starts to share more and how the dialogue becomes more profound and engaging.

After the conversation, take a moment to reflect on

how it went. How did the other person respond to your open-ended questions? What did you learn about them that you didn't know before? How did it affect the dynamics of the conversation?

This exercise will improve your use of open-ended conversation questions, leading to more meaningful interactions and stronger relationships. Practice regularly, and you'll soon notice how your conversations become more profound and enriching.

<u>Exercise 4:</u>
**Practice Asking Follow-Up Questions**
Practice asking follow-up questions to improve your ability to engage in deeper conversations. When someone shares something with you, build on what they've said by asking questions and encouraging them to elaborate.

For example, if a friend mentions, *"I've started going to the gym,"* you could follow up with, *"What motivated you to start working out?"* or *"How are you feeling after your first few sessions?"* These questions show you're actively listening and interested in their new routine and motivation.

Another example could be if someone says, *"I've just started reading a new book,"* you might ask, *"What's it about?"* or *"What made you choose that particular book?"* These follow-up questions allow them to share more about their interests and thoughts, leading to a more engaging conversation.

Lastly, if a person says, *"I'm going to a big family event this weekend,"* you could ask, *"What kind of event is it?"* or *"Is there something you're especially looking forward to at the party?"* This shows you're curious about their experiences and invites them to share more.

Using follow-up questions can create more natural and in-depth conversations. Practice this in daily conversations and observe how it leads to more meaningful and exciting interactions.

### Exercise 5:
### Transition Back to Lighter Topics

It's important to recognize when a conversation is reaching a point where the other person might need a break or a shift in focus.

Sometimes, this is necessary to maintain the flow of the conversation or to create a more balanced and pleasant atmosphere.

Try finding natural ways to change the subject, such as saying, *"I can tell it's been a tough time for you. Has there been anything that's given you a little relief or joy during this period?"* or *"That sounds like a heavy experience. Is there something you've done to care for yourself through it all?"* Practice making these transitions with empathy and respect for the other person's feelings.

<u>Exercise 6:</u>
**End the Conversation in a
Positive and Meaningful Way**

Ending a conversation well is just as important as starting it. A successful conclusion leaves both parties with a sense of satisfaction and a positive experience.

As you approach the end of a conversation, you can start signaling this by summarizing the key points discussed or by expressing gratitude for the conversation. For example, you might say, *"It's been really great talking with you about this. I appreciate you sharing your thoughts,"* or *"Thank you for telling me about your project. I look forward to hearing how it develops."*

If time is running out or the conversation feels like it's reached its natural conclusion, you can use a friendly closing like, *"It was great talking with you. I hope you have a wonderful day,"* or *"I've got to go now, but I've really enjoyed our chat."*

Practice ending conversations in different contexts—both personal and professional. Notice how different endings affect the tone and lingering impact of the conversation. Afterward, reflect on what worked well and how to improve your technique in future interactions. By becoming more mindful of how you end conversations, you can ensure that your interactions always leave a positive impression and strengthen your relationships.

# The Role of Humor: When and How to Use It Effectively

Even when we're skilled at navigating conversations and building deeper relationships, there's another element that can add an extra layer to our interactions: humor. Humor isn't just a tool to lighten the mood; it's also a powerful way to connect, break down barriers, and create a sense of community.

Humor acts like social glue. It entertains, helps us connect with others, builds trust, and fosters a relaxed atmosphere. When we laugh together, our bodies release endorphins, the natural feel-good hormones, reducing stress and giving us a sense of well-being. By incorporating humor into our conversations, we can forge stronger bonds, ease tensions, and make our interactions more memorable and enjoyable.

Using humor may seem challenging, especially if we're worried about how our attempts at being funny will be received. Many people think we must be natural comedians who use humor, but it's more about being relaxed and attuned to everyday life's small, funny moments. A simple, humorous comment or self-deprecating humor can lighten the mood and create a stronger connection.

Humor can be a powerful tool both at work and in personal life. At work, a funny remark during a meeting can lighten the mood and help colleagues feel more comfortable. For example, we might say, *"I think the coffee machine is the hardest worker in the office,"* which could get everyone to laugh and relax. If technology is acting up during a meeting, we could joke, *"Looks like the computer needs more coffee than we do today!"* These little moments of humor can break the tension and create a more relaxed atmosphere.

Choosing the right humor in our communication is essential for respecting and fostering an inclusive environment. Humor based on shared experiences can unite people and create community. For example, at work, we might say, *"Can we add an extra day between Saturday and Sunday? I think we could all use more weekends!"* It's a lighthearted comment that makes people laugh without offending anyone.

In personal settings, a joke at the dinner table can bring the family closer and help everyone unwind. For instance, we could say, *"Remember when we tried setting up the tent in the backyard, and it took us three hours? We had more fun with the instructions than the actual camping trip!"* Humor doesn't have to be perfect or planned; it's about finding small moments to bring a smile to others.

Humor is also an effective way to handle challenges. It can provide a psychological buffer against stress and adversity, making it easier to face challenging situations. For example, it can help to joke with a friend after a long, hard day: *"I had so much work today, I thought I'd accidentally taken on a second job!"* Or if we're facing a daunting task, we could say, *"This project is like a marathon—I'm not sure if I'll make it to the finish line, but I'm taking it one mile at a time!"* By including humor in our daily lives, we promote a healthier and happier mindset for ourselves and those around us.

Using humor in sensitive situations requires a delicate balance. It's vital that humor never diminishes the seriousness of the topic or distracts from essential messages. However, when used thoughtfully, humor can ease the tension and make difficult conversations more accessible and less intimidating. For example, if we're talking to a stressed friend about work, we might say, *"We're so good at working hard. We should get medals for it!"* This can make them smile and maybe feel less pressured. If a friend shares that they've had a rough day, we could say, *"Sounds like you've had one of those days where a pause button would come in handy."* This acknowledges their feelings while bringing a smile to their face.

Self-deprecating humor can effectively address personal flaws, encouraging others to share their experiences. For instance, if we're clumsy, we might say, *"I'm so good at tripping over my own feet, I should consider becoming a professional acrobat."* This shows we can laugh at ourselves, making others feel more comfortable sharing their small mistakes and flaws. However, being respectful and mindful of how others react is essential. If the humor doesn't land well or unintentionally offends, we should be ready to adjust our approach.

On the other hand, exclusive humor—often involving sarcasm, teasing, or jokes at someone else's expense—can make people uncomfortable, offended, or hurt. It's crucial to avoid jokes that target someone's race, gender, ethnicity, religion, or other personal traits. The key is to choose humor that uplifts and unites rather than creates distance or discomfort.

If we're unsure whether a joke is appropriate, it's better to skip it. It's safer to take a more neutral approach than to risk hurting or offending someone. By being mindful of our words and how they might be received, we can ensure that our humor contributes positively to the conversation and strengthens our relationships.

Humor is a powerful tool in communication that can build bonds and lighten the mood in conversations.

To practice using humor effectively, start by observing the small, funny moments in your daily life. Jot these moments down in a notebook and practice sharing them with others. Begin with simple and harmless comments, and pay attention to the reactions of the people you're speaking with. Adjust your approach to ensure your humor uplifts and connects rather than causing discomfort.

You can also incorporate self-deprecating humor by sharing small, funny stories about yourself. This can create a relaxed atmosphere and encourage others to share their experiences. By practicing these techniques, you'll gradually become more comfortable using humor as an effective communication tool.

## The Art of Giving Compliments: Genuine Praise

The ability to give compliments can have a remarkable impact on our relationships. Compliments, like humor, can uniquely strengthen bonds and lift spirits. Giving a compliment requires more than just saying something kind—it's about expressing our appreciation sincerely rather than out of obligation. When we offer thoughtful, genuine compliments, we show others we see and value them, which can help create more profound and meaningful connections.

However, it's important to remember that our body language and tone of voice play a significant role when giving compliments. We should make eye contact and use a warm tone to ensure our compliment is sincere. Doing so can genuinely uplift others and foster a positive atmosphere around us.

## The Key to Great Compliments

For a compliment to feel genuine, it should be specific and tied to the person's real quality or action. General statements like *"You're amazing"* are nice to hear but often feel superficial. Instead, we should focus on specific traits or actions of the person.

For example, *"Your ability to organize and execute the event with such attention to detail made a difference."* This makes the compliment more meaningful and reinforces the behavior or qualities we genuinely appreciate in the person.

Timing is also crucial. A compliment given at the right moment— after someone has achieved something or made a noticeable effort— can feel more relevant and impactful.

For example, if a colleague has just finished a presentation, we could say, *"Your presentation was really clear and inspiring. It was obvious that you put a lot of work into it."*

After an enjoyable dinner, for example, we might say to a friend, *"Your ability to make everyone feel welcome and relaxed is amazing. It makes our time together so much more special."*

A genuine compliment comes from the heart and shows that we truly appreciate the other person's efforts or qualities. By being specific and choosing the right timing, we can make our compliments more effective and meaningful.

## THE KEY TO GREAT COMPLIMENTS

Practice giving specific compliments. Choose someone in your life—a colleague, friend, or family member—and focus on a particular trait or action you appreciate.

Write a concrete and precise compliment, and say it to the person in an appropriate context. For example, if it's for a friend, you could say, *"I really appreciate how you always take the time to listen, when I need to talk. Your support and understanding mean a lot to me."* This shows that you value their kindness and empathy in your relationship.

**Compliments in Social Settings**
Practice giving compliments in social settings where it can help strengthen your relationships. At the next social

event you attend, choose someone and find something specific to compliment them on. The host's hospitality or a friend who helped organize the event. For example, you might say, *"I'm really impressed by how well you organized the evening. Everyone's had a fantastic time, thanks to you."*

**Write and Give Compliments**
Take a few minutes daily to write down what you appreciate about the people around you. Based on these observations, try to give at least one compliment daily. This practice will help you become more aware of the positive qualities in your relationships and train you to provide meaningful and effective compliments.

These exercises will improve your ability to give sincere, specific, and well-timed compliments. This will enhance your communication skills, strengthen your relationships, and create a more positive atmosphere around you.

## Avoid Common Pitfalls

While the intention behind giving a compliment is usually positive, there are certain pitfalls to be mindful of. Excessive praise can make compliments feel insincere. If we constantly compliment someone, the compliments may lose their impact or come across as flattery.

For example, continually telling a colleague they're doing a fantastic job might eventually feel superficial. Choosing compliments carefully and ensuring they are specific and thoughtful is better. Praise someone for something concrete, like how they handled a difficult situation calmly and professionally. This shows that we've genuinely noticed and appreciated their effort, making the compliment more meaningful and authentic.

Another pitfall is focusing on the wrong aspects, especially those outside the person's control, such as physical features. Complimenting these traits can feel inappropriate and superficial. For instance, saying, *"You have such beautiful eyes"* to a colleague in a professional setting may feel entirely out of place.

Instead, focus on compliments, recognizing the person's effort, skills, or character. A more appropriate compliment might be, *"I'm really impressed by your presentation skills; it was clear and persuasive."* This shows appreciation for something the person has worked hard on and can take pride in.

By being aware of these pitfalls, we can ensure that our compliments always feel genuine and valued.


## Compliments Across Cultures

Compliments can be perceived very differently across cultures. In some cultures, direct praise, especially in public, may cause embarrassment or discomfort; in others, it may be expected and appreciated. Understanding these cultural differences is essential to ensure our compliments are respectful and appropriate.

For example, in many Asian cultures, compliments are expected to be deflected or downplayed to avoid appearing boastful. In such situations, being mindful and respectful of these norms is essential.

Instead of publicly giving big compliments, we may choose a more discreet way to express our praise, which is more appropriate and respectful.

Observing how people around us give and receive compliments can be helpful. We can also ask about local customs and norms in the cultural contexts we find ourselves in. This ensures that our compliments align with cultural expectations. For example, if we work with colleagues from different cultural backgrounds, we can notice how they react to praise and adjust our approach accordingly. If a colleague from a culture where modesty is valued does a great job, we might give a private compliment such as, *"I just wanted to say that your efforts made a difference today. Thank you for your hard work."* This way, we avoid putting them in an uncomfortable situation.

By being culturally sensitive, we can ensure our compliments are always well-received and help us build stronger, more respectful relationships.

Although compliments and constructive feedback seem very different, they share an essential common thread: both are about building and maintaining strong relationships through communication. While compliments strengthen relationships by acknowledging and appreciating the positive qualities of others, constructive feedback is about helping them grow and improve. They are two sides of the same coin—one uplifts, and the other guides.

## Giving Constructive Feedback

Whether we're giving feedback in a meeting room or over coffee with a friend, feedback is vital to personal and professional growth.

When used wisely, feedback can refine our skills and strengthen our relationships.

Constructive feedback serves as a mirror, reflecting our strengths and the blind spots we may not know. When we view feedback as an essential part of our development, we can transform the often uncomfortable experience of criticism into a valuable opportunity for personal and professional growth. Giving feedback effectively involves what we say and how we say it. For feedback to be effective, it must be clear, specific, and focused on a behavior or action that the person can change or adjust.

Imagine we're leading a project team and notice that Alex, one of the team members, tends to rush through presentations and often leaves out important details. Instead of saying, *"Alex, your presentations are always rushed,"* we can take a more constructive approach: *"Alex, I've noticed that in your recent presentations, some important details were missing that could have given us a clearer picture. Could you take some time to include those in your next presentation?"* This approach is specific and straightforward and provides a direct action for improvement.

In a personal situation, our partner often forgets to inform us about plan changes. Instead of saying, *"You always forget to tell me about changes,"* we could take a more constructive approach: *"I've noticed that sometimes there are changes in our plans that I don't hear about. It would really help if you could update me immediately to avoid confusion."* Again, this approach is specific and offers a direct path for improvement.

Empathy plays a crucial role in delivering constructive feedback. It means understanding and considering the feelings of the person receiving the feedback. It doesn't mean avoiding the truth but rather phrasing the input to show respect and consideration for the person's effort and feelings. By acknowledging the value of the person's work before addressing areas for improvement, we help maintain their self-esteem and motivation, which can encourage them to accept and act on the feedback more positively.

## GIVING CONSTRUCTIVE FEEDBACK

Choose a person you frequently interact with, whether at work or in your personal life. Think about a situation where you've observed something that could be improved or where there is potential for growth. Write down how you would clearly and precisely formulate this feedback. Ensure that your feedback focuses on the issue and includes suggestions on what the person can do differently.

Find an opportunity to talk with the person about a neutral topic. During the conversation, focus on listening without interrupting. Ask follow-up questions to show that you are genuinely interested in what the person is saying. This will create an open and trusting atmosphere where you can naturally give feedback.

After listening actively and understanding the person's perspective, present your feedback. Use the notes you

prepared and choose your words carefully. Begin with a
positive observation, then move on to the specific feedback, and conclude with a suggestion for action. Be sure
to frame your feedback to show you understand their
situation and want to support their improvement.

After delivering the feedback, take some time to reflect
on how the conversation went. How did the person
react? Was your feedback clear and helpful? Is there
anything you could have done differently? Write down
your observations so you can learn from the experience
and improve your skills in the future.

Completing this exercise will strengthen your ability to
listen actively, give empathetic and constructive feedback, and reflect on your communication skills. This
will help you improve your relationships and support
others' personal and professional growth.

## Receiving Feedback

Receiving feedback is crucial to our personal and professional development, but it can also be challenging. Often, feedback can feel
like criticism of our efforts, which can be difficult to manage. This
feeling is widespread when the feedback is vague and lacks focus on
specific actions or behaviors.

Without clear action points for improvement, feedback can easily be
perceived as a personal critique rather than constructive guidance.

For example, if someone says to us, *"You need to be more efficient,"* without specifying the concrete actions we can take to achieve that, it can be hard to know how to respond, leaving us feeling attacked or inadequate. This type of feedback provides no clear direction on how we can improve, making it feel more like a judgment of our character rather than help for our growth.

On the other hand, if the feedback is specific, such as, *"I've noticed that tasks are often delayed due to a lack of prioritization. Perhaps you could try making a daily to-do list to keep track of your deadlines,"* it becomes clear what changes we can make and how we can improve. This makes accepting the feedback as constructive support rather than criticism more accessible.

When receiving feedback, it's essential to consider whether it is concrete, focuses on behavior or actions, and offers clear improvement steps. If any of these elements are missing, we can ask for specific examples or suggestions for improvement. By receiving feedback with this openness and clarity, we can better understand what is expected of us and use the feedback to enhance our skills and development.

Using these strategies in our daily conversations improves our ability to give and receive feedback effectively and helps create an environment of mutual respect and continuous improvement. When we are mindful of the types of feedback that genuinely help us and communicate our needs clearly, we contribute to a culture where feedback becomes a positive and constructive force in our relationships and work lives.

# Asking for Help: Strategies for Success

Asking for help, whether for a work project or personal support, can often feel like admitting a weakness. Many of us are influenced by societal norms that equate independence with strength, leading us to see asking for help as a sign of vulnerability. However, shifting our perspective and view asking for help as a strength can make a huge difference. It shows we are committed to achieving the best outcomes by involving others' expertise and viewpoints. Acknowledging that we cannot handle everything alone in a complex world is the first step toward changing how we view and approach asking for help.

When we ask for help, we must articulate our request clearly and choose the right time. We should be specific about the assistance we need. Vague requests can create confusion and result in us not getting the help we need, which may discourage us from seeking help in the future.

Instead of saying, *"I need help with this project,"* we could try something more precise, like, *"Could you help me review the budget section of this project next Thursday?"* This makes it easier for others to understand how they can assist and shows respect for their time and abilities.

Similarly, rather than saying, *"I need help around the house,"* we can say something more specific, like, *"Could you help me prepare dinner on Friday so we can spend more time together afterward?"* This clearly outlines the need, respects the other person's time, and creates a positive experience for both parties.

It's also essential to ask for help well in advance. This gives others time to provide the necessary assistance and shows that we've planned instead of leaving things until the last minute. For example, if we need help organizing a family gathering, rather than saying, *"Can you help with the party?"* we could be more specific by saying, *"Could you help me arrange the seating and decorate the living room for the party on Saturday?"* This clarifies the type of help needed and when required, making it easier for the person to say yes and plan their time accordingly.

Being specific and timely in our requests increases our likelihood of receiving the help we need effectively and respectfully.

## ASKING FOR HELP: STRATEGIES FOR SUCCESS

Asking for help effectively requires us to be specific in our requests.

**Be Specific and Clear**
Practice making your requests clear and precise. Identify a situation in your daily life where you need help and phrase your request with as many details as possible. Instead of saying, *"I need help with my presentation,"* try, *"Can you help me prepare for Monday's meeting by reviewing my slides and giving feedback by Friday?"*

Practice saying it aloud to yourself or a friend so it feels more natural when asking for help in real-life situations.

### Plan Your Request in Advance

If you know you'll need help moving some furniture over the weekend, you might say, *"Hey, could you help me move the couch on Saturday? I want to plan ahead so it works with your schedule."* This shows you respect their time and allows them to plan and prepare.

### Develop and Maintain Your Network

Consider who in your network you can ask for different types of help. Create a list of colleagues, mentors, friends, and family members and note the assistance each can provide. For example, a colleague might help with professional guidance, a mentor could offer strategic advice, and a friend or family member might provide emotional support. Practice contacting these individuals regularly and offering your help to keep these relationships strong and reciprocal.

By incorporating these exercises into your daily routine, you'll improve your ability to ask for help and strengthen your relationships through clear and respectful communication. This will make it easier for you to receive the support you need while contributing to a more robust, more supportive network.

## Handling Rejection When Asking for Help

Even when we make our requests clear and respectful, we may still experience rejection when asking for help. This is a natural part of life, and how we handle rejection can significantly impact our future willingness to seek assistance. It's important to remember that a rejection does not necessarily reflect our worth or relationship with the person we asked. There are many reasons someone might be unable to help—they may be busy, lack the resources, or feel they aren't equipped to assist in that particular situation.

When we receive a rejection, we must respond with understanding and gratitude for the honest answer. You could say, *"Thank you for being honest about that. I understand you have a lot on your plate right now."* This shows respect for their situation and prevents us from taking the rejection personally. Maintaining a positive attitude ensures the relationship remains strong and open for future interactions.

It's also helpful to reflect on the rejection and consider whether there's anything we can learn from the situation. Perhaps we could have phrased our request differently, chosen a better time, or maybe the person simply wasn't the right one to ask. These reflections can help us adjust our approach in the future and increase our chances of receiving the support we need.

Handling rejection constructively also strengthens our resilience and adaptability. It reminds us that we can find solutions and alternative paths, even when we face challenges. By viewing rejection as part of our learning process and an opportunity for growth, we can stay motivated and continue seeking help when needed without letting the fear of rejection hold us back.

# WITH YOUR REVIEW

Thanks for reading "How to Talk to Anyone." We hope you've already found some tips and tools that are helping you connect more easily and confidently in your conversations.

If you've enjoyed the book so far, we'd love to hear your thoughts! Taking a moment to leave a review can really help others discover how this book can make a difference for them, too. Your feedback means a lot and helps us continue to create valuable content.

Many people find themselves in the same situation you once were—eager to improve their communication skills and connect more confidently with others. Our goal with "How to Talk to Anyone" is simple: to make mastering the art of conversation easy and accessible for everyone.

This is where your voice matters. While some may pick a book by its title or cover, most rely on reviews to help them decide.

So, for those looking to overcome social anxiety, build meaningful relationships, and feel more at ease in conversations, we ask:

Could you take a moment to share your review?

Your review, which takes just a minute, could help...

- One more person build stronger connections.
- One more friend feel more confident in social settings.
- One more professional succeed in conversations.
- One more family member feel truly heard.
- One more dream of meaningful relationships come true.

## Ready to make a difference?

To do this, simply find the book on Amazon's website
(or wherever you purchased it from) and locate
the section to leave a review. Choose a star rating and
write a couple of sentences.

You can find the book on Amazon by scanning this QR code:

With heartfelt thanks,
C. Holmbaeck and R. Eskildsen

P.S. If you think this book could help others improve their communication skills, please share your knowledge of it with them. They'll appreciate it, and you might inspire them to make positive changes too!

# Chapter 4

# EFFECTIVE COMMUNICATION AND CONFLICT MANAGEMENT

We all encounter situations where our boundaries are pushed or crossed, leading to frustration and discomfort. Setting clear boundaries is crucial for maintaining healthy relationships and protecting our well-being. Whether in our professional lives or personal relationships, communicating our boundaries respectfully and confidently is essential in avoiding unnecessary conflicts and strengthening our connections. In this chapter, we will explore how to improve our ability to set limits and handle the challenges that arise, when those boundaries are tested.

# Setting Clear Boundaries

When we struggle to communicate our boundaries clearly, it can have severe consequences for our mental and emotional well-being. If our boundaries are repeatedly crossed, it can lead to stress and burnout. It can also damage our relationships, as we may begin to feel taken advantage of or undervalued by those around us. For example, we might say yes to too many tasks at work, because we don't want to disappoint our colleagues, or we may allow friends or family to constantly demand our time and energy, even when we need a break. This can create a vicious cycle, where we withdraw and become less willing to engage in social interactions, further isolating ourselves and worsening our overall well-being.

Fortunately, learning to set boundaries is more accessible than we often fear, once we understand how to do it. By learning to establish boundaries and respectfully address potential resistance, we can prevent situations from escalating into conflict and help maintain positive, strong relationships.

We've all experienced situations where we felt our boundaries were crossed. Perhaps a colleague asked us to take on a last-minute task, or a friend overstepped our boundaries by showing up unannounced. These moments can cause discomfort and frustration, but they also present opportunities to practice setting clear and healthy boundaries.

This chapter explores various strategies and techniques for setting boundaries in our professional and personal lives. We'll examine how to recognize when our boundaries are being crossed, and how to communicate our needs assertively and respectfully. By learning to set and maintain boundaries, we can create healthier, more balanced relationships and improve our quality of life.

# Understanding Personal Boundaries

Personal boundaries are the invisible lines we draw around ourselves to protect our sense of self and well-being. They define who we are, what we're comfortable with, and what we're not. These boundaries can manifest in different ways, including emotional and physical boundaries. Emotional boundaries are about who we confide in and how much of our inner life we share with others.

We might only share our deepest feelings and thoughts with close friends or family, while keeping conversations more superficial with acquaintances and colleagues. These boundaries help us protect our emotions and prevent us from getting hurt or taken advantage of.

Physical boundaries are our personal space, and they determine how close we allow others to get to us and what we're comfortable with in terms of touch. For example, we might feel uncomfortable if someone stands too close or touches us without permission. By setting clear physical boundaries, we can ensure that our personal space is respected.

Understanding and setting these boundaries are essential for maintaining healthy relationships and a strong sense of self. Knowing our limits and communicating them clearly to others can prevent misunderstandings and conflicts.

Without clear boundaries, we can quickly feel overwhelmed, taken advantage of, or drained. These feelings often arise when our boundaries aren't respected. For example, we might experience stress and exhaustion if we constantly say yes to others' requests, even when we lack time or energy. Setting and maintaining boundaries protects our well-being and ensures we have the time and energy to care for ourselves.

We can imagine a situation with a colleague who constantly interrupts us with minor tasks. Not setting a boundary can lead to stress and inefficiency. But by saying, *"I'm happy to help you, but I need to finish this task first,"* we protect our time and well-being. Or, if we think about a friend who calls late at night when we really need to relax, we could say, *"I'd love to talk with you, but could we do it earlier in the day?"* In this way, we set a boundary that protects our rest time.

Personal boundaries are necessary not only to protect ourselves but also to ensure healthy and respectful relationships.

## Setting Boundaries Through Communication

Setting and expressing our boundaries clearly and confidently is crucial, though this can sometimes feel challenging. First, we must understand our boundaries and make clear decisions about what is and isn't acceptable. The key to setting boundaries is using "I" statements without feeling guilty or needing to apologize.

For example, our boundaries are often tested at work, especially regarding overwhelming workloads. If our boss asks us to take on another large project, when we are already swamped, we could say, *"I appreciate your trust in my abilities, but I already have several important projects that require my full attention. Can we prioritize which tasks should come first or find another solution?"* This approach ensures our workload remains manageable, allowing us to produce quality work without feeling overwhelmed.

Boundaries are often challenged in personal life, particularly in close relationships. If a friend frequently shows up unannounced but we value our privacy and alone time, we could say, *"I really appreciate that you want to spend time together, but I need to plan my schedule. Can we agree on a time that works for both of us?"* This allows us to protect our time and space without damaging the friendship.

Boundaries can also be tested in families, especially when there is an expectation to attend every family event. If we are invited to a gathering but need time or have other plans, we might say, *"I really appreciate the invitation, but I need a day to rest and recharge. I'd love to join next time."* This shows respect for our family's wishes while prioritizing our own needs.

There are also general situations where boundaries may be crossed, such as excessive physical contact. If someone is too physically close and invades our personal space, we could say, *"I need a bit more space around me. Can we continue the conversation with a little more distance?"* This ensures that interactions remain respectful and comfortable for both parties.

If we receive inappropriate comments or jokes, we can say, *"That comment makes me uncomfortable. I'd appreciate it if we could keep the conversation respectful."* This helps maintain a respectful and pleasant atmosphere in our interactions.

We protect our sense of self and well-being by setting clear and respectful boundaries. Clear communication about our boundaries allows us to manage our relationships confidently and respectfully, whether at work or in our personal lives. Remembering that it's perfectly acceptable to enforce our boundaries and insist that others respect them is essential.

When we are consistent and clear, we create an environment where our needs are met, and our relationships become stronger and healthier.

## When Our Requests Aren't Respected

If our boundaries aren't respected, taking further steps to protect our well-being is crucial. When someone repeatedly crosses our boundaries despite communicating our needs, we may need to re-evaluate how we handle that relationship moving forward.

First, we should calmly reiterate our boundaries. We can say, *"I've mentioned that I feel uncomfortable with [specific situation]. It's important to me that you respect this boundary."* It's essential to remain consistent and firm without becoming aggressive.

If our boundaries continue to be violated, we might say, *"I've explained before that it's important for me to have time to myself in the evenings. I'd appreciate it if you could respect that, and we can talk later."* By being transparent and calm, we reinforce our needs without escalating the situation into a conflict.

If repeated efforts to communicate our boundaries don't lead to changes in behavior, we might need to consider distancing ourselves from the relationship, if possible. While this can be difficult, especially in professional or family settings, our mental and emotional well-being should always be our top priority.

We can also seek support from others, who respect our boundaries and can help us navigate the situation. This might include a trusted friend, colleague, or professional like a therapist. They can offer advice and support, helping us find new ways to manage challenging relationships.

Remembering that we have the right to protect our boundaries and health is essential. Standing firm on our boundaries, even when they aren't respected, sends a strong message about self-respect and self-worth. It shows that we value ourselves and our needs, which can inspire others to do the same in their lives.

## Respecting Others' Boundaries

While setting our boundaries is important, respecting the boundaries of others is equally crucial. This mutual respect is fundamental for building trust and understanding in all relationships. We respect others' boundaries by actively listening and listening to their cues.

We must be aware of verbal and nonverbal signals that might indicate discomfort. Verbal signals could include a change in tone, such as a more hesitant or nervous voice, vague answers, or pauses in conversation. If someone begins responding briefly or avoids answering questions, this can also be a sign of discomfort.

Nonverbal signals are just as important to observe. If someone steps back, crosses their arms, avoids eye contact, or looks around, they may be feeling uncomfortable or trying to withdraw from the conversation. Recognizing these signs helps us understand when we might be overstepping someone's boundaries and adjust our behavior accordingly.

If we're unsure whether we're crossing a boundary, it's perfectly acceptable to ask clarifying questions. For example, we might ask, *"Are you comfortable talking about this topic?"* or *"Is it okay if I call you after work?"* These questions show that we respect the person's well-being and avoid crossing their boundaries.

Respecting others' boundaries shows that we value their comfort and sets a standard for how we expect our boundaries to be treated. For instance, if a friend says they don't want to discuss personal matters at work, we can respect that by keeping conversations professional. Similarly, if a colleague requests not to be contacted outside of work hours, we respect their wish by only reaching out during office hours.

By respecting others' boundaries, we create a culture of mutual respect and understanding, which strengthens relationships and helps ensure that our boundaries are respected in return.

## Adjusting Boundaries in Close Relationships

Our boundaries can easily blur in close relationships—whether with family, friends, or a romantic partner. Maintaining clear boundaries often becomes more challenging as we grow closer to someone. It's important to understand that boundaries in close relationships must be flexible and can change over time.

For example, the boundaries we set at the beginning of a friendship or relationship may shift as we get to know each other better and build trust. What felt appropriate in the beginning can be adjusted as the relationship evolves. This requires a willingness to renegotiate and adapt our boundaries to fit our current needs and desires.

Regular conversations are crucial in close relationships. By discussing what works and what can be improved, we can prevent minor frustrations from growing and keep the relationship healthy. Asking each other questions like, *"How do you feel about our communication?"* or *"Is there anything you'd like to change in how we spend time together?"* allows both people to feel heard and respected.

These conversations also make it easier to adjust boundaries as our needs or circumstances change.

For example, if we're going through a tough time and need more support, we might say to our partner: *"I've been feeling pretty overwhelmed lately and could really use some extra support. Could we make time to talk every evening this week?"* This shows we value our partner's support while taking responsibility for our needs.

Or, if a colleague frequently interrupts us while we're working, we could say: *"I appreciate your interest, but I need some uninterrupted time during these hours. Can we discuss this later, when I'm finished?"* This communicates our need for focus while maintaining a positive relationship with the colleague.

If a family member criticizes our choices, we could say: *"I understand you're concerned, but I need you to respect my decisions. I've considered them a lot, and they're important to me."* This acknowledges their concern while standing firm on our own choices and needs.

By being open and honest about our needs and listening to the needs of our partners or friends, we can create a balance that strengthens our relationships. It helps prevent minor irritations from becoming more significant conflicts and ensures the relationship remains balanced and built on mutual support and understanding.

## Tips for Strengthening Your Boundaries in Daily Life

Setting healthy boundaries is crucial for maintaining your mental and emotional balance. By putting theory into practice, you can protect your time, energy, and well-being in a way that strengthens your relationships. These strategies will guide you in applying what you've learned, helping you effectively set and maintain your boundaries and improving your quality of life and relationships.

## Be Specific and Clear

It's essential to communicate your boundaries clearly and precisely. Instead of giving vague responses, be specific about what you need. For example, say, *"I can't take on any more tasks right now,"* instead of saying, *"I'm too busy."*

## Communicate with Respect

When setting boundaries, do so in a way that respects your and others' feelings. By being assertive without being aggressive, you can ensure your message is understood without creating conflict. For example, say, *"I need some time alone to recharge,"* instead of, *"Leave me alone."*

## Be Consistent

Consistency is vital in maintaining your boundaries. Follow your boundaries, and don't let others repeatedly cross them. If you've set a boundary, stick to it and remind others of it when necessary.

## Listen to Your Feelings

Your feelings often indicate, when your boundaries are being crossed. If you're feeling frustrated, overwhelmed, or taken advantage of, it's a sign that you may need to set a boundary. It's essential to listen to these feelings and act on them.

## Practice Saying 'No'

Saying no can be difficult, but it's essential to set boundaries. Practice saying no in a kind but firm way. For example, say, *"I can't attend the meeting today,"* instead of making excuses or overloading yourself.

## Prepare for Pushback

When setting boundaries, you may face resistance from others who are used to you saying yes to everything. It's essential to be prepared for this and stand firm in your boundaries, even if it feels uncomfortable.

## Give Yourself Permission

It's important to remember that it's okay to set boundaries. You have the right to protect your time, energy, and well-being. Permit yourself to prioritize your own needs without feeling guilty.

## Communicate Boundaries Early

It's best to set your boundaries before a situation escalates. By communicating your boundaries early, you can prevent misunderstandings and conflicts. For example, tell your colleagues you need at least a day's notice before taking on new tasks.

By following these strategies, you can learn to set and maintain healthy boundaries, which can help you create more balanced relationships and improve your overall quality of life.

# Quick and Effective Handling of Misunderstandings

Misunderstandings can quickly arise if we use unclear language or have different expectations in a conversation. For example, if we tell a colleague, *"I need the report soon,"* they might think *"soon"* means in a few days, while we mean today.

Another example could be when we're planning the weekend with our partner. We say, *"Let's go on a trip,"* our partner assumes we mean a short drive when we've planned a full-day outing. By being mindful of how we phrase things and clarifying any potential misunderstandings immediately, we can prevent minor issues from becoming more significant problems. This helps ensure more precise and more effective communication.

## Asking Clarifying Questions

If we need more certainty about something in a conversation, addressing the situation before it becomes a potential misunderstanding is essential. A helpful approach is to repeat what the other person has said in our own words and then ask clarifying questions. This shows we're engaged and want to ensure we're both on the same page.

For instance, if we've arranged to meet a friend for lunch but are unsure about the time, we could say, *"Just to confirm, we're meeting at 12 at the café, right?"* This helps clarify the details and avoid confusion later.

When facing potential uncertainties, asking questions like, *"Could you clarify what you mean by 'immediate action' in this context?"* or *"What are your expectations for the team by the end of this phase?"* can be incredibly helpful. These questions reveal differences in understanding and ensure everyone is aligned on what needs to be done.

For example, if we're planning a family outing and are unsure who is responsible for the food, we can ask, *"Just to clarify, you're handling lunch, and I'll take care of the drinks. Is that correct?"* By addressing these details early on, we can prevent minor uncertainties from growing into more considerable misunderstandings.

## Handling Misunderstandings

When we encounter a misunderstanding, patience, openness, and clear communication are required to resolve it effectively. The first step is acknowledging that confusion has occurred without placing blame. For example, we can say, *"It seems there's been a misunderstanding. Let's clear it up."* This helps set a constructive and collaborative tone.

For instance, if we are working on a project with a colleague and realize that both of us have been working on the same tasks, leading to wasted time and duplicate efforts, instead of blaming our colleague, we might say, *"It looks like there's been a misunderstanding about who was handling which parts of the project. Let's clarify this so we can avoid it in the future."* We can then discuss how tasks were divided and why the mix-up occurred.

Working together to find a solution, such as more precise task assignments and regular check-ins, can help ensure we are on the same page moving forward.

Similarly, at home, if we and our partner discussed taking a weekend trip but both assumed the other would arrange the accommodations, this could lead to confusion as the weekend approaches. Instead of getting frustrated, we could say, *"It seems like there was a misunderstanding about who was booking the accommodations. Let's figure it out together."* By acknowledging the confusion without assigning blame, we can quickly resolve the issue, whether finding a last-minute place to stay or rescheduling the trip with more explicit roles next time.

Once we identified the cause of the misunderstanding, the next step is to work together to find a solution or compromise that addresses everyone's needs and concerns. We can agree on specific steps to prevent future misunderstandings, such as regular discussions and more transparent communication.

## Tips for Handling Misunderstandings Quickly and Effectively

When aiming to avoid and swiftly resolve misunderstandings, it's essential to have practical strategies in place.

### Be aware of the causes

Remember that misunderstandings often arise from unclear language, assumptions, or differing expectations. Be mindful of these causes from the start of any conversation.

### Ask clarifying questions

If you sense a misunderstanding, ask questions to clarify. For instance, when planning dinner with a friend and you're unsure about the meeting time, you can ask: *"Just to confirm, we're meeting at 6:00 PM at the restaurant, right?"* or *"Should I bring dessert, or are we picking something up on the way?"*

### Repeat and seek confirmation

Restate what the other person has said in your own words, to ensure you've understood correctly. For example, when discussing weekend plans with your partner, repeating their suggestion helps confirm you're both on the same page.

If your partner says, *"I was thinking we could go to the beach on Saturday, and then visit my parents in the afternoon,"* you can paraphrase: *"So we're heading to the beach in the morning and visiting your parents afterward, right?"* This gives them a chance to confirm or adjust the plan.

### Summarize at the end of discussions

Wrap up conversations by summarizing the main points to ensure everyone is on the same page. This helps clear up any immediate misunderstandings and prevents future ones.

### Acknowledge confusion without blaming

When a misunderstanding occurs, acknowledge it without assigning blame. For example, you can say: *"It seems like a misunderstanding. Let's find a solution together."* This keeps the tone positive and collaborative.

### Discuss perspectives openly

Share your viewpoints to discover where the disagreement or confusion arose. This will help clarify any misunderstandings and prevent similar issues in the future.

### Find solutions or compromises

Once you've identified the root of the misunderstanding, work together to find a solution or compromise that meets everyone's needs. You can agree on clear steps to avoid future misunderstandings, such as holding regular conversations and improving communication clarity.

### View misunderstandings as learning opportunities

Use misunderstandings as a chance to learn. Reflect on why the misunderstanding happened, what contributed to it, and how it was resolved. For example, if a friend shows up at the wrong time for a meeting, you could think, *"I learned that I need to be more precise when setting times, and in the future, I'll confirm times in writing to avoid confusion."* This will help improve your communication in the future.

By following these strategies, you can resolve misunderstandings more effectively, strengthen professional and personal relationships, and foster transparent, effective communication.

## Managing Disagreements Without Escalating Tension

Disagreements are a natural part of human interaction. They can stem from different opinions, misunderstandings, or conflicting goals. The issue isn't the disagreement itself but how we handle it. When we understand what causes conflicts to escalate, we can manage the situation much better. Often, conflicts intensify when we feel threatened, misunderstood, or dismissed. We can make a significant difference by recognizing these feelings early in a conversation.

For example, if we notice our shoulders tensing up or our breathing becoming faster, these can be signs that we feel pressured or defensive, which could lead the disagreement to escalate. Being aware of these signals early allows us to take steps to stay calm and handle the situation more constructively.

## Strategies for Handling Disagreements

Effectively managing disagreements to prevent escalating is vital to maintaining harmony in our relationships. One effective strategy is to use neutral language to avoid placing blame and focus on the facts. For example, instead of saying, *"You never listen to me,"* we could say, *"I feel like I'm not being heard."* This small change can prevent the other person from becoming defensive and keep the conversation constructive. Maintaining a calm and steady tone also helps us manage the situation better. Our tone can convey empathy and understanding, which often helps reduce tension.

If a colleague at work becomes upset over a project change, we can say, *"I see that you're frustrated by this change. Let's work together to find a solution."* Or if a friend feels hurt by something we said, we might say, *"It wasn't my intention to hurt you. Can we talk about how I can explain it better?"* Using these approaches, we handle disagreements in a way that fosters understanding rather than conflict.

As mentioned in chapter 2, page 30, active listening is central to de-escalating conflict. It's about truly hearing what the other person is saying, reflecting on their feelings, and confirming our understanding. For example, *"It sounds like you're really frustrated, because you feel your ideas aren't being considered. Is that right?"* This approach shows that we acknowledge the other person's feelings, making them more open to finding a resolution together. Using these strategies, we can manage disagreements in a way that keeps communication open and respectful, prevent tensions from escalating, and help maintain strong, healthy relationships.

## Focusing on Shared Goals

One effective strategy for resolving disagreements is shifting the focus from different viewpoints to a shared goal. For instance, in a family situation, if a conflict arises over how tasks are divided, we can remind our partner that our shared goal is to create a harmonious home, where both of us feel valued.

Instead of blaming each other for not doing enough, we can discuss how to distribute tasks more fairly to achieve our mutual goal. By avoiding personal attacks and focusing on collaboration, we create an atmosphere where both parties feel heard and respected, and together, we can find a solution that benefits everyone.

Another example might be a conflict with a friend about how often we should meet. If one person wants to get together more frequently than the other, we can focus on the shared goal of maintaining a strong and healthy relationship. Instead of insisting on our needs or getting frustrated with different expectations, we can talk about how to find a balance that works for both of us. For instance, we might agree to meet once a week, but also be open to spontaneous plans when convenient for both. By focusing on the common goal of preserving and strengthening the friendship, we can find a solution that considers both perspectives.

Focusing on a shared goal is a powerful way to resolve conflicts and find solutions that satisfy everyone involved. Shifting the focus from individual needs to what we want to achieve together creates a more collaborative and positive environment. It's about listening to each other, being flexible, and working toward a solution that strengthens our relationships.

## Tips for Handling Disagreements

It's helpful to have strategies to handle disagreements without escalating tension.

### Use Neutral Language

Avoid placing blame. Instead of saying, *"You always do things your way,"* try saying, *"I've noticed we sometimes approach things differently."* This can open up a more constructive dialogue and reduce the chance that the other person feels attacked or defensive.

### Maintain a Calm and Steady Voice

When speaking, it helps to maintain a calm tone. This can convey empathy and understanding, which often helps lower tension. A quiet tone also allows you to stay in control of the situation.

### Practice Active Listening

When listening to the other person, repeat their concerns in your own words to show that you genuinely understand them. For example, you could say, *"It sounds like you're concerned about how this change will affect our schedule. Is that right?"* By showing that you acknowledge their concern, you create space for a more constructive conversation where both of you feel heard.

### Focus on Shared Goals

Shift the focus from your different viewpoints to a common goal. If you disagree about allocating your budget, for instance, focus on the fact that both of you want financial stability and security. Instead of insisting on individual priorities, consider which expenses are most important for both of you in achieving financial security and shared future goals, such as saving for a trip or building an emergency fund.

By focusing on securing your shared finances, you can find a budget balance that accommodates your needs and wishes.

### Avoid Personal Attacks or Criticism
Try to avoid getting personal or critical. Instead, focus on understanding each other's viewpoints and working together to find a solution.

### Collaborate on Solutions
Once you've understood the cause of the disagreement, work together to find a solution or compromise. Focus on shared goals and collaborate to find the best path forward.

### Avoid Dismissing Each Other's Ideas Without Consideration
Take time to carefully consider each other's ideas before dismissing them. This will foster a more solution-oriented atmosphere and help you find options that meet your needs. By following these tips, you can manage disagreements more effectively, prevent tension from escalating, and build stronger professional and personal relationships.

# Handling Criticism: Moving from Defense to Improvement
Sometimes, we find ourselves in situations where the other person

isn't trying to be helpful but resorts to making hurtful comments or personal attacks. This can happen professionally and personally and can be particularly challenging to handle. When we encounter such situations, we must have strategies to respond while maintaining our composure and dignity.

The first step is recognizing when the conversation shifts from being constructive to becoming destructive. This shift is often evident, when the other person begins to attack us personally rather than discussing the issue objectively.

In professional settings, for example, a colleague may criticize our work with disparaging remarks like, *"You're always so slow"* or *"Your work is never good enough."* Comments like these do not contribute to a constructive dialogue but erode confidence and create a hostile atmosphere.

A manager might also deliver personal attacks during feedback sessions by saying things like, *"You have a bad attitude"* or *"You're not reliable,"* instead of focusing on specific areas for improvement.

In personal relationships, it can be even more difficult. A friend or family member might attack our character by saying things like, *"You're always so selfish"* or *"You only think about yourself,"* rather than discussing the current issue. They may also bring up past events, such as *"You're never dependable. Remember last time you promised to help and didn't show up?"* This drags past problems into the present and makes it difficult to resolve the current issue.

Although it can be tempting to react defensively when faced with personal attacks, it's essential to consider the consequences of this reaction. Defending ourselves against hurtful remarks can trap us in a negative cycle where the conversation becomes even more heated and destructive.

# Effective Strategies for
# Handling Personal Attacks

When we recognize signs of personal attacks, disparaging comments, or a focus on past actions, we can choose to take a deep breath and stay calm. It's natural to feel hurt or angry, but responding in a way that doesn't escalate the conflict is crucial. A good starting point is acknowledging the other person's feelings without accepting the hurtful comments. For example, if a colleague says something negative about our work, we can respond by saying, *"I can see that you're frustrated, and I'd like to understand what's concerning you."* This shows we're willing to listen and engage in a constructive conversation without accepting personal attacks.

In personal relationships, if a friend or family member begins criticizing our character during a discussion, we can say, *"I hear that you're upset, but let's focus on how we can solve the current issue together."* Responding this way keeps the conversation centered on the problem and reduces the risk of the situation spiraling out of control.

Another strategy is to steer the conversation back to a more constructive track. If things go off the rails, we can say, *"I want to find a solution to this issue. Can we talk about how we can improve things going forward?"* This shifts the focus from the negative to the positive and helps de-escalate the conflict.

If the hurtful comments persist, it's essential to set boundaries. We can say something like, *"This conversation is becoming uncomfortable. Let's take a break and revisit it later when we're both calmer."* This gives both parties time to reflect and cool off, which can prevent the situation from escalating further.

By recognizing when a discussion is turning toxic and using these strategies, we can navigate difficult conversations gracefully, maintain control, and ultimately work towards solutions that foster growth rather than conflict.

## Dealing with Persistent Attacks

We must protect ourselves and prioritize our well-being when faced with ongoing hurtful comments or personal attacks. Speaking with a trusted friend or family member who can offer support and perspective can be incredibly comforting and empowering. Sharing our experiences with someone who listens without judgment and truly understands can help us process our emotions and feel validated.

If the situation feels too challenging to manage alone, seeking external help might be necessary. In professional settings, this could involve a manager or HR department for support in addressing workplace issues. Personal relationships include seeking a therapist or counselor who can offer tools to navigate the challenges and provide a neutral perspective to help restore balance in our relationships.

Maintaining our boundaries is crucial, especially when faced with persistent pressure or attacks from others. By consistently upholding our boundaries, we demonstrate respect for ourselves and our needs while sending a clear message about what is acceptable behavior. This clarity helps prevent misunderstandings and reduces the likelihood of others attempting to overstep our limits. Being firm in our approach creates a stable framework for our relationships, making it easier for others to understand and respect us. This is vital for maintaining self-esteem and staying strong professionally and personally.

If someone continues to disregard our boundaries, we must recognize that the issue lies with them, not in our right to protect ourselves. Standing firm in our boundaries is crucial to maintaining self-respect and ensuring we don't lose faith in our judgment.

## When It's Necessary to Step Away

Sometimes, the healthiest choice is to step away from someone, who repeatedly harms us through hurtful comments and personal attacks. This decision can be difficult, especially if it involves a close relationship, but it's crucial for our mental and emotional well-being. Choosing to step away doesn't mean giving up or avoiding conflict; it means protecting our boundaries and, in doing so, protecting ourselves.

Constant exposure to negativity can have damaging effects on our self-esteem and well-being. Continuing to engage with someone who doesn't respect our boundaries can lead us to internalize their criticism and start doubting our self-worth. Over time, this can result in stress, anxiety, and even depression.

Recognizing when enough is enough is critical. We may take a break from the relationship by reducing contact or, if necessary, cutting ties altogether. This could involve avoiding social gatherings where the person is present or calmly communicating that we need time to safeguard our well-being.

Stepping away from a harmful relationship is an act of self-respect and self-care. It sends a strong message to ourselves and others that our boundaries must be respected and that our well-being is a top priority. By making this challenging but necessary choice, we allow ourselves the space to heal and rebuild our self-esteem and emotional health.

# Tips for Handling Criticism:
# From Defense to Improvement

When faced with criticism, responding in a way that promotes understanding and growth rather than conflict can be challenging. Here are some strategies to help you navigate criticism effectively:

## Recognize Destructive Criticism

It's essential to identify when a conversation shifts from constructive to destructive. This happens when the other person starts attacking you personally rather than addressing the issue objectively.

## Stick to the Facts

Instead of getting defensive, try steering the conversation back to the original issue. For example, you might say, *"Let's focus on the current situation and find a solution."*

## Take a Break if Needed

Pausing to keep your cool is okay, if the conversation becomes too heated. You can say something like, *"I feel like this conversation is becoming too personal. Let's take a break and return when we can talk more constructively."*

## Set Clear Boundaries

If hurtful comments persist, it's essential to set boundaries. For example, you can say, *"This conversation is becoming uncomfortable. Let's pause and revisit it when we're both calmer."*

## Avoid Defensive Reactions

Defensiveness can often be perceived as a counterattack, which might escalate the conflict. Instead of defending yourself against personal attacks, focus on understanding the other person's perspective. For example, *"I can see you're frustrated. Let's talk about how we can improve the situation."*

## Acknowledge Emotions Without Accepting the Attack

A good approach is acknowledging the other person's feelings without accepting hurtful remarks. For example, you could say, *"I hear that you're upset, but let's concentrate on how we can resolve the current issue together."*

## Redirect the Conversation to Constructive Dialogue

If the conversation spirals out of control, you can say, *"I'd like to find a solution to this problem. Can we focus on how we can improve things moving forward?"*

## Involve a Third Party in Persistent Attacks

If the attacks remain ongoing and destructive, it may be necessary to involve a third party. In the workplace, this could mean bringing in a manager or HR. In personal relationships, you might involve a mutual friend or a counselor.

## Stand Firm with Your Boundaries

It's crucial to remain consistent with your boundaries and avoid sending mixed signals. This shows respect for yourself and your needs, reducing the likelihood of others taking advantage of you.

## Withdraw if Necessary

If someone continually hurts you with personal attacks and hurtful comments, it may be necessary to step back from the relationship to protect your mental and emotional well-being.

By following these guidelines, you can handle criticism more effectively, avoid escalating conflicts, and build stronger professional and personal relationships.

# Chapter 5

# STRENGTHEN RELATIONSHIPS WITH THE 5 LOVE LANGUAGES

After exploring practical techniques for meaningful conversations, we're ready to improve our communication skills. What if we could better understand what strengthens and sustains our most important relationships? This is where the concept of the five love languages comes into play.

Imagine how much our relationships could improve if we truly understood how our loved ones prefer to receive and express love. Gary Chapman, a well-known author and marriage counselor, identified five primary ways people intensely experience love. These love languages are words of affirmation, quality time, receiving gifts, acts of service, and physical touch.

Love isn't limited to romantic or intimate relationships. The profound love and connection we share can also exist between close friends and family members. Platonic and familial love are just as essential and can be as powerful as romantic love. We can express and receive love in various ways, regardless of the type of relationship. Using the five love languages to show love to friends and family strengthens our bonds and creates more profound, meaningful connections. It's a reminder that love is a universal emotion that enriches every part of our lives, not just the romantic ones.

In this chapter, we'll explore the five love languages and provide practical advice on how to apply them in our everyday lives. Whether you want to enhance your relationship with your partner, strengthen your bond with your children, or deepen your connections with friends, this insight will help you communicate in ways that truly matter.

## A Detailed Description of Each Love Language

A deep understanding of the five love languages allows us to tailor our communication and actions to have the most significant positive impact on our relationships. When we know how those closest to us feel most loved and appreciated, we can strengthen our bonds and create a more harmonious and satisfying connection. In this section, we will explore each love language in depth so that we can apply it purposefully in our everyday lives.

## Words of Affirmation

Words of affirmation are the first of the five love languages, meaning we verbally express love, praise, and recognition. This love language can enhance any relationship—whether with friends, family, or a spouse—by making us feel seen and appreciated. When we primarily communicate through words of affirmation, we feel most loved and valued when we receive verbal expressions of support and praise.

Examples of words of affirmation range from simple compliments to encouraging words and expressions of gratitude. For instance, a remark like, *"You look amazing today,"* can lift someone's mood and boost their self-confidence, whether directed at a friend, family member, or spouse. Similarly, saying something like, *"I really appreciate you cleaning the kitchen,"* acknowledges the person's effort and helps them feel valued and loved.

Regularly expressing words of affirmation can create a positive and supportive atmosphere in all our relationships. It's essential to remember that these words must be genuine and heartfelt. When we offer praise or acknowledgment that we truly mean, it can significantly impact the recipient's emotional well-being and strengthen our bond. Whether with friends, family members, or a spouse, words of affirmation can be a powerful way to express our love and appreciation.

## Quality Time

Quality time is the second of the five love languages, and it centers on spending uninterrupted, meaningful time together. This love language shows that we value the other person's company and prioritize time together, creating a sense of closeness and intimacy. For individuals whose primary love language is quality time, the most important thing is to feel seen and heard through shared, meaningful experiences.

Examples of activities that express this love language include going for walks, where we can talk and enjoy each other's company or having deep conversations without distractions from electronic devices. Setting aside regular times to be together is also an effective way to show that we value time with those we care about. It could be as simple as cooking a meal with a friend, playing a game with a family member, or sitting down to discuss the day's events with a partner.

The key to speaking this love language is being fully present and engaged in the moment. It's not about the quantity of time spent but the quality of that time. By creating these moments of focus and presence, we strengthen the bonds in our relationships and demonstrate to our friends, family, and partners how much they mean to us.

## Receiving Gifts

Receiving gifts is the third of the five love languages and serves as a symbolic way to show love. Gifts represent thoughtfulness and attention because they show that we've been thinking of each other and want to bring joy. For those whose primary love language is receiving gifts, the value of the gift is not necessarily what matters most but rather the thought and care behind it.

Examples of gifts expressing this love language could be a bouquet given without a specific reason, or a book we know they've mentioned. It could also be small, personalized items that show we know and understand them, like their favorite chocolate or a handwritten note with a loving message. For friends, it might be a small souvenir from a trip, and for family members, it could be something home-made or an item that holds special meaning in the relationship. Most importantly, the gift shows we've been thinking of and appreciate them.

Gifts don't have to be expensive or extravagant to hold significance. It's the thought behind the gift that counts. Giving a gift is a tangible way to express love, and it can create a sense of joy and connection. By being mindful of the little things that can bring happiness to our friends, family, and partners and regularly surprising them with thoughtful gifts, we can strengthen our relationships and show how much they mean to us.

## Acts of Service

Acts of service are the fourth of the five love languages, and they involve showing love through actions and helpful tasks. This love language demonstrates that we are willing to support and assist our loved ones, which can create a deep sense of care and attention. For those whose primary love language is acts of service, practical help and support often mean more than words or gifts.

Examples of acts of service that express this love language include taking care of household tasks such as cooking, cleaning, or doing the laundry. Small acts of service in everyday life, like making coffee in the morning, running errands, or helping with practical matters, can also have a significant impact. For our friends, it could mean helping with a task or a project; for our family members, it might involve taking care of daily chores or supporting them in their activities. These actions show that we are attentive to their needs and are willing to lighten their burdens.

Performing acts of service requires attentiveness and the initiative to step in where we can make a difference. It's about recognizing where help is needed and acting on it. By regularly offering our help and support through tangible actions, we show our love practically and meaningfully. This can strengthen our relationships by fostering a sense of mutual dependence and care. When we engage in acts of service that matter to our friends, family, and partners, we demonstrate how much we value and love them.

## Physical Touch

Physical touch is the final of the five love languages, focusing on creating connection and security through physical closeness. This love language shows that we value each other's physical presence, which can enhance feelings of safety and togetherness. For those whose primary love language is physical touch, feeling physically close to friends, family, and partners is essential to feeling loved and appreciated.

Examples of physical touch that express this love language include hugs, kisses, holding hands, and general physical presence. Sitting close together, giving a comforting pat on the shoulder, or simply touching our partner's arm can have great significance. For friends, it might be a friendly hug or a pat on the back, and for family members, it could be resting a hand on their shoulder or offering a warm embrace during a conversation. These small gestures show that we are attuned to each other's need for physical contact and willing to meet that need.

Physical touch creates a sense of connection that can be comforting and empowering. It's a way to communicate love without words and can be especially important when verbal communication may not be enough. Regularly incorporating physical touch into our daily inter-actions with friends, family, and partners can forge deeper emotio-nal connections and strengthen our relationships. Physical touch is a powerful way to show that we are there for our loved ones physically and emotionally.

Understanding and communicating in each other's love languages is essential, fostering a more profound sense of appreciation and un-derstanding in our relationships. By mastering the art of speaking the love languages in our various relationships, we become better equipped to meet each other's emotional needs and strengthen our bonds. Communicating in a way that truly resonates with our friends, family members, or partners helps avoid many misunder-standings and conflicts that often arise in relationships.

## A Brief Overview of the Five Love Languages

Understanding and knowing the five love languages can help us strengthen our relationships with partners, family, friends, or even colleagues.

### Words of Affirmation

For those whose love language is words of affirmation, feeling most loved and appreciated comes through praise, encouragement, and verbal acknowledgment. Compliments and affirming remarks make us feel seen and valued.

### Quality Time

If quality time is our love language, we feel most loved when we spend meaningful, undistracted time together. It's about presence, deep conversations, and shared experiences that foster connection and intimacy.

### Receiving Gifts

For those who have gifts as their love language, it's not the gift's monetary value but the thought and attention behind it that matters. Receiving a gift shows that we are on someone's mind and appreciated, creating a sense of joy and connection.

### Acts of Service

When acts of service are our love language, we feel most loved when others perform helpful or supportive actions for us. Practical assistance shows care and attention, building a deep sense of appreciation and love.

### Physical Touch

If physical touch is our love language, we feel most loved through physical closeness, such as hugs, kisses, and holding hands. Physical contact provides comfort, security, and emotional connection.

These love languages are essential for improving communication and strengthening bonds across all relationships.

## Identifying Our Own and Others' Love Languages

Identifying our own and others' love languages is vital to improving relationships with friends, family, and partners. It requires observation and reflection to understand how we and those we care about best receive and express love.

### Discovering Our Love Language

One way to discover our love language is by considering how we typically express love to others. How we show affection and appreciation can often reveal our own love language.

For instance, if we frequently offer compliments and encouraging words to our friends, family, or partners, our love language may be words of affirmation. If we prioritize spending quality time with others, whether through planning get-togethers or simply being present, our love language could be quality time.

If we enjoy giving gifts, picking out thoughtful items, or creating personalized presents, our love language might be receiving gifts. If we often help others with daily tasks like cooking, cleaning, or offering support on projects, our love language could be acts of service. Physical touch is likely our love language, if we feel joy in physical contact, such as hugging, holding hands, or being physically close.

By examining what we give to others, we gain insight into what is most meaningful to us, which can help identify our love language. Another approach is to observe ourselves in various situations. How do we feel when someone compliments us? What's our reaction when spending quality time with loved ones? How do we feel when receiving a small gift or when someone helps with a task? How do we respond to physical touches like hugs or hand-holding? Paying attention to our emotional responses in these moments can offer valuable clues about what makes us feel most loved and appreciated.

This self-awareness is essential for communicating our needs clearly and building more robust, meaningful relationships with the people we care about.

## Discovering the Love Languages of Those Close to Us

To identify the love languages of our friends, family members, or partners, we can begin by observing their behavior and needs. What do they ask for most often? What do they express they're not getting enough of?

For example, if a friend frequently expresses joy over small gifts, like when we bring them their favorite snack, their love language might be receiving gifts. If a family member often seeks our help with tasks like cooking or cleaning and seems to appreciate when we do things for them, their love language could be acts of service. Or, if our partner mentions not spending enough time together and enjoys shared activities like walks or watching movies, their love language is likely quality time.

Similarly, if a friend regularly seeks affirmation and lights up when we praise or acknowledge their efforts, their love language may be words of affirmation. And if a family member frequently hugs us or seeks physical contact, like putting an arm around our shoulder, their love language might be physical touch.

We can gain insight into our loved one's primary love language by paying attention to what they seem to miss or what makes them feel most appreciated.

The same applies to children. To discover our child's love language, we can observe their behavior and reactions. If a child often brings us drawings or small gifts, their love language could be receiving gifts. If they constantly want us to play with them or spend time together, their love language might be quality time.

If they always offer to help around the house or appreciate when we do something for them, their love language may be acts of service. If they frequently seek praise and are happy when we compliment their achievements, their love language could be words of affirmation. And if they often seek physical contact, such as hugging or holding hands, their love language is likely physical touch. By paying attention to these signs, we can better understand our children's needs and strengthen our relationships by speaking their love language.

Understanding the love languages of those close to us allows us to create deeper and more meaningful connections. When we know what makes our loved ones feel valued and appreciated, we can tailor our actions and communication to meet their needs. Using this knowledge in everyday life helps us show love and care that truly resonates with those we cherish, leading to greater understanding, fewer misunderstandings, and a stronger connection in our relationships.

## Improving Close Relationships Through Love Languages

Once we've identified our own and others' love languages, we must adjust our behavior to communicate more effectively and strengthen our relationships. By speaking love languages in a way that resonates with each individual, we can create a more profound sense of connection and understanding.

### Using Love Languages in Everyday Life

To adapt our approach, we can start by incorporating love languages into our daily interactions with those closest to us. This involves being mindful of what makes our friends, family members, partners, or children feel loved and valued and tailoring our actions accordingly.

For someone who values words of affirmation, we should offer daily compliments or express gratitude. For example, we could tell a friend, *"I love the energy you bring to our friendship,"* or *"You look great today."* For family members, we could say, *"Thank you for helping with dinner; it really means a lot to me."*

 To a partner, we might say, *"I appreciate how you always support me."* For a child, we could say, *"I'm so proud of how hard you worked in school,"* or *"I love when you help at home."* These small acknowledgments can significantly impact those who feel loved through words.

If quality time is their love language, we can plan regular activities or conversations where we can be fully present without distractions. This could mean setting up weekly coffee dates or walks together for friends. For family members, it could be scheduling a regular activity like playing a game or watching a movie together.

For a partner, it might mean having a weekly date night focused on fully engaging with each other. For children, it could mean spending time playing, reading, or going on an outing.

For those who appreciate gifts, thoughtful gestures that show we're thinking of them can make a big difference. For friends, we might pick up a small item we know they'll love, such as a book or a little souvenir. For family members, surprising them with their favorite treat can be meaningful. For a partner, small gifts like flowers or chocolates can show that they're on our minds. For children, it could be a small toy, their favorite snack, or a handmade card.

If acts of service are their love language, we should look for ways to help them daily. For friends, this might mean offering to help with a practical task like moving or fixing something at their home.

We can take care of household chores such as cooking or doing the dishes for family members. We can help partners with their daily responsibilities to lighten their load. For children, this could involve assisting with homework, tidying their room, or preparing their school things.

For those who value physical touch, simple gestures like a hug or a friendly touch on the arm can be meaningful. For friends, this might involve giving them a hug when we greet or say goodbye. For family members, a hand on the shoulder during a conversation can convey warmth. Holding them or sitting close during a movie can foster a connection for a partner. It might be hugging children when they get home from school or tucking them in at night.

It's also crucial to be consistent and genuine in our actions, demonstrating that we truly appreciate and love them. We can strengthen our daily connections by establishing habits and regular activities that align with their love language. Surprising them with small gestures of affection, such as an unexpected gift or spontaneous act of kindness, can make a significant difference and show our care meaningfully.

By speaking the love language that resonates most with our loved ones, we can nurture more robust, healthier relationships rooted in genuine understanding and appreciation.

## Tips for Using Love Languages in Everyday Life

Once you've identified your and your loved ones' love languages, you can tailor your actions to strengthen relationships and create deeper connections and understanding.

## Words of Affirmation

If your close relationships value words of affirmation, regularly expressing appreciation and praise for their efforts and qualities is vital. For example, you could tell your partner: *"I really appreciate how you always take the time to listen to me."* When talking to a friend, you might say: *"You have an amazing ability to make me feel better, no matter what I'm going through."* You could acknowledge your children's efforts with: *"I'm really impressed by how hard you work on your homework."* And when speaking to your parents, you could say: *"Thank you for always supporting me—it means so much to me."*

## Quality Time

If your partner values quality time, you could plan a weekend getaway where you both disconnect and enjoy each other's company. For friends who appreciate time together, you could arrange a monthly dinner date where you try a new restaurant or cook together at home. For children who love quality time, you could establish a weekly game night where you play their favorite games and engage in their world. For parents who cherish quality time, you could plan a cozy monthly Sunday lunch where you cook together and discuss life, memories, and plans.

## Gifts

For your partner who appreciates gifts, surprising them with thoughtful gestures—both big and small—can be impactful. It could be something as simple as a handwritten letter expressing your feelings or a special card with a heartfelt message. For friends who love gifts, you might find something unique that speaks to their interests, like a special coffee blend for a coffee lover or a quirky plant for a plant enthusiast. For children who appreciate gifts, you could create a little "treasure hunt" with surprises like colorful stickers, fun pencils, or a book from their favorite series. For parents who enjoy receiving gifts, a nostalgic item like a framed family photo or a collection of their favorite music from their youth could be meaningful.

## Acts of Service

When your partner values the act of service, showing care by taking on small tasks that will ease their day can make a big difference. For friends whose love language is acts of service, offering help with something they need, like running errands or assisting with a project, can show your support. For family members who appreciate acts of service, you can offer help with tasks they find challenging. Regarding children, acts of service might involve doing something extra for them, like helping with homework or preparing a special breakfast, showing that you're attentive to their needs.

## Physical Touch

If your partner appreciates physical touch, you can express love by holding them close when you see them, taking their hand as you walk together, or giving them a comforting hug after a tough day. For friends who feel loved through physical contact, showing care by placing a hand on their shoulder, giving a warm hug when you meet, or sitting close to watching a movie or chatting can mean a lot. For family members who value physical touch, a hug when you greet, say goodbye, or sit close during a conversation can convey your affection.

When it comes to children, physical touch might include hugging them when they get home from school, playing with their hair while talking about their day, or holding them close when they need comfort.

It's essential to be consistent and genuine in your actions to show that you genuinely appreciate and love those around you. Surprises and spontaneous acts of affection can demonstrate your care in meaningful ways. You build more profound and fulfilling relationships by consistently showing love and appreciation in ways that resonate with your loved ones.

## Sharing What Matters Most to Us

When we express our love language, we must be clear and specific so that those close to us truly understand what matters most. This clarity can foster a stronger emotional connection and ensure we feel seen and appreciated.

If words of affirmation are our love language, we might say: *"It makes me happy when you notice the small things I do, like cooking or tidying up. Hearing your acknowledgment means a lot to me."* We could tell a friend: *"It really means a lot when you compliment my ideas and initiatives."* To family members, we might say: *"I appreciate it when you notice the little things I do for you."* And to a partner, we could say: *"I love it when you compliment me on what I do for us."*

If quality time is our love language, we could express: *"I feel really close to you when we spend time together, just the two of us without distractions. It would mean a lot to me if we could have a night each week dedicated to just being together."* To a friend: *"I really enjoy our time together, and I'd love to have more uninterrupted moments with you."* For family: *"It means a lot to me when we set time aside to be together without distractions."* To a partner: *"It would be wonderful if we could have a weekly evening just to spend time together."*

If receiving gifts is our love language, we might say: *"I love getting little gifts because they show me that you're thinking about me. It doesn't have to be anything big—something simple like a flower or chocolate makes me really happy." To a friend: "It means a lot to me when you surprise me with a small gift." To family members: "I'm thrilled when you give me little things that show you've thought of me." And to a partner: "I love it when you surprise me with small gifts; it shows me that you're thinking of me."*

*If acts of service are our love language, we could express: "I feel really appreciated when you help me with small tasks at home. It makes my day easier and shows me how much you care." To a friend: "I'm pleased when you lend a hand with practical things." To the family: "It means a lot to me when you help me with household tasks." To a partner: "I love it when you help me with daily chores because it really shows your care."*

*If physical touch is our love language, we could say: "I feel really close to you when we are physically affectionate. Something as simple as holding or hugging me makes a big difference." To a friend: "I feel closer to you when we sit next to each other and share a moment." To the family: "I love when we give each other a comforting pat on the back or a hug." And to a partner: "Physical closeness, like holding me or a hug, means a lot to me."*

Being open and honest about our love language helps our loved ones better understand and meet our needs, creating a more harmonious and fulfilling relationship where everyone feels loved and appreciated.

## Challenges and Solutions

We may face challenges while learning and applying love languages, but solutions are available to overcome them. One common challenge is knowing our or others' love languages. This can lead to misunderstandings and feelings of being underappreciated. To solve this, self-reflection and open conversations with loved ones are essential. We can ask them what makes them feel loved and share our preferences.

Another challenge is adjusting our behavior to meet someone else's love language, which can feel unnatural or awkward, especially if it's very different. The solution here is to take small steps and gradually incorporate these new habits into daily life. For example, if your partner's love language is physical touch and it's not something you naturally do often, start with small gestures like hugging them in the morning or a gentle touch on the arm when you pass by.

Consistency can also be challenging. It's easy to slip back into old habits, especially when stressed or busy. To counter this, we can remind ourselves of the importance of expressing love in the way that matters most to our loved ones. Setting reminders or making a list of small actions we can do daily can help ensure we keep speaking their love language.

Another potential hurdle is not constantly receiving the response we hope for, even when we try to speak our loved one's love language. This can lead to frustration, but it's important to remember that changing dynamics in a relationship takes time, and our efforts won't always yield immediate results. By being patient and showing love and care, we will strengthen the relationship over time.

Being open and honest about our love language helps loved ones better understand and meet our needs, leading to more harmonious and fulfilling relationships where everyone feels loved and appreciated. Though it may be unfamiliar and even challenging to use love languages, especially if they don't come naturally, taking small steps and staying consistent will lead to positive changes in relationships. As we experience the benefits of deeper connection and greater mutual understanding, we'll be motivated to continue speaking love's language, ultimately strengthening our bonds with those we care about.

## Tips for Overcoming Challenges When Using Love Languages

You may encounter various challenges when trying to understand and apply love languages. You can build more profound, meaningful relationships by being mindful of these obstacles and working through solutions.

### Lack of Awareness of Love Languages

Challenge: One common issue is that you may still need to be made aware of your own or others' love languages, which can lead to misunderstandings and feelings of being unappreciated.

Solution: Reflect on your own needs and those of your loved ones. Have open conversations about what makes each of you feel loved. Ask direct questions like, *"How do you feel most valued in our relationship?"* or *"What do I do that makes you feel loved and important?"* These conversations help reveal preferences and needs, making it easier to connect in ways that matter most.

### Changing Behavior Feels Unnatural

Challenge: It might feel awkward to change your behavior to match someone else's love language significantly, if it differs greatly from yours.

Solution: Take small steps and gradually incorporate new habits into your daily life. For example, if your partner's love language is physical touch and doesn't come naturally to you, start by holding their hand while watching a movie or offering a gentle shoulder squeeze as you pass by. Small, meaningful gestures can slowly become a natural part of your interactions.

## Maintaining Consistency

Challenge: It's easy to fall back into old habits, especially when stressed or distracted by other things.

Solution: Remind yourself of the importance of expressing love in the way that matters most to your loved ones. Set reminders or create a list of small, daily actions you can take to ensure you continue speaking their love language consistently.

## Lack of Immediate Response

Challenge: Sometimes, even when trying to speak your loved ones' love languages, you may not receive the response you're hoping for, leading to frustration or discouragement.

Solution: Be patient and keep showing love and care. Shifting the dynamics of a relationship takes time, and your efforts won't always yield immediate results. Trust that your consistent care will strengthen the relationship over time.

Approaching these challenges with openness and persistence can strengthen your relationships and achieve a deeper emotional connection. This will make your relationships more harmonious and fulfilling, and ensure that you and your loved ones feel loved and valued in ways that truly resonate.

# Conclusion

Communication is one of the most fundamental skills shaping our personal and professional lives. Throughout this book, we've explored various aspects of effective communication, from handling criticism constructively and navigating complex conversations to understanding and applying the five love languages.

We've seen how clear and respectful communication can strengthen relationships, reduce misunderstandings, and create an environment where collaboration naturally thrives.

Criticism and feedback are inevitable elements of daily interactions. Learning to handle them effectively can transform them from sources of stress into opportunities for growth. By separating emotions from facts, asking clarifying questions, and setting goals based on feedback, we can improve our skills and build resilience against negative feedback.

Misunderstandings and disagreements are also part of communication dynamics. We can navigate these challenges without escalating tensions by repeating and summarizing, asking clarifying questions, and focusing on common goals. Mastering these techniques helps maintain harmony and fosters a spirit of collaboration in both personal and professional relationships.

Understanding and applying the five love languages can enhance our relationships by adjusting how we express and receive love to match individual needs. This applies not only to romantic relationships but also to those with friends, family, and colleagues. Words of affirmation, quality time, gifts, acts of service, and physical touch are all essential elements that can enrich our interactions and create deeper connections.

Communication is a lifelong learning process that requires continuous attention and practice. With the right tools and resources, we can keep improving our communication skills, building stronger relationships, and creating more meaningful and effective interactions. Communicating respectfully and empathetically is vital to success and fulfillment, whether at work, home, or social settings.

# References

First Impressions | Psychology Today
*https://www.psychologytoday.com/us/basics/first-impressions#:~=Often%2C%20someone's%20first%20impression%20is,person%20who%20has%20a%20babyface*

Effective Conversation Starters: 10 Tips to Break the Ice
*https://www.holstee.com/blogs/mindful-matter/effective-conversation-starters-10-tips-to-break-the-ice*

How to Teach Social Skills Through Role-Playing
*https://blog.esc13.net/how-to-teach-social-skills-through-role-playing*

Active listening: The key of successful communication
*https://www.ncbi.nlm.nih.gov/pmc/articles/PMC4844478/*

Body Language and Nonverbal Communication
*https://www.helpguide.org/articles/relationships-communication/nonverbal-communication.htm*

How to Understand Body Language and Facial Expressions
*https://www.verywellmind.com/understand-body-language-and-facial-expressions-4147228*

Cialdini's 6 Principles of Influence - Definition and examples
*https://conceptually.org/concepts/6-principles-of-influence*

Using Emotional Intelligence to Improve Communication
*https://www.ddiworld.com/blog/emotional-intelligence-and-communication*

Emotional regulation: Skills, exercises, and strategies
*https://www.betterup.com/blog/emotional-regulation-skills*

Empathy: A Cornerstone of
Effective Communication and Connection
*https://everydayspeech.com/blog-posts/general/empathy-a-cornerstone-of-effective-communication-and-connection/*

Sympathy vs. Empathy: What's the Difference?
*https://www.verywellmind.com/sympathy-vs-empathy-whats-the-difference-7496474*

How to Find a Mentor for Communication Skills Development
*https://www.linkedin.com/advice/o/how-can-you-find-mentor-who-help-develop-your-communication-boote*

Positive Daily Affirmations: Is There Science Behind It?
*https://positivepsychology.com/daily-affirmations/*

Healthy Communication Tips - Relationships
*https://www.verywellmind.com/managing-conflict-in-relationships-communication-tips-3144967*

Conflict Resolution in Relationships & Couples: 5 Strategies
*https://positivepsychology.com/conflict-resolution-relationships/*

5 Conflict Resolution Strategies
*https://www.pon.harvard.edu/daily/conflict-resolution/conflict-resolution-strategies/*

10 Tactics for Working with Difficult People
*https://managementtraininginstitute.com/10-tactics-for-working-with-difficult-people/*

Effective Communication in High-Stress Situations
*https://achievecentre.com/blog/effective-communication-in-high-stress-situations/*

Fear of public speaking: How can I overcome it?
*https://www.mayoclinic.org/diseases-conditions/specific-phobias/expert-answers/fear-of-public-speaking/faq-20058416*

Applying The 5 Love Languages To Daily Life
*https://medium.com/writers-blokke/applying-the-5-love-languages-to-daily-life-458b694b6f0e*

How to Stay Emotionally Connected
in a Long Distance Relationship
*https://marryfromhome.com/blog/how-to-stay-emotionally-connected-in-a-long-distance-relationship/*

How to Improve Your Relationships by
Making the Best Compliments
*https://betterhumans.pub/how-to-improve-your-relationships-by-making-the-best-compliments-607076ce6c1c*

How to ask for help | Psyche Guides
*https://psyche.co/guides/how-to-ask-for-help-without-discomfort-or-apology*

Make 'Em Laugh: How Humor Can Be the Secret Weapon in Your Communication
*https://www.gsb.stanford.edu/insights/make-em-laugh-how-humor-can-be-secret-weapon-your-communication*

Cultural Differences in Business Communication - John Hooker
*https://johnhooker.tepper.cmu.edu/businessCommunication.pdf*

Bridging Generational Divides in Your Workplace
*https://hbr.org/2023/01/bridging-generational-divides-in-your-workplace*

8 Effective Networking Strategies for Professionals
*https://www.indeed.com/career-advice/career-development/networking-strategies*

Negotiation Strategies: Top Strategies for Negotiation
*https://www.vistage.com/research-center/business-growth-strategy/six-successful-strategies-for-negotiation/*

The Importance of Celebrating Milestones - Maryville Online
*https://online.maryville.edu/blog/importance-of-celebrating-milestones/*

Emojis influence emotional communication,
social attributions, and information processing
*https://www.sciencedirect.com/science/article/abs/pii/S0747563221000443*

Effective Email Communication - UNC Writing Center
*https://writingcenter.unc.edu/tips-and-tools/effective-e-mail-communication/*

7 Communication Failure Examples (With Definition) - Indeed
*https://www.indeed.com/career-advice/career-development/communi-cation-failure-example#:~ =Business%20leaders%20can%20learn%20 from,strategies%20to%20enhancing%20their%20practices*

10 Communication Goals With S.M.A.R.T. Examples
*https://clickup.com/blog/communication-goals/*

A New Approach to Building Your Personal Brand
*https://hbr.org/2023/05/a-new-approach-to-building-your-personal-brand*

Video conferencing etiquette:
10 tips for a successful video conference
*https://resources.owllabs.com/blog/video-conferencing-etiquette*

28 Best Practices for Email Etiquette in the Workplace
*https://www.indeed.com/career-advice/career-development/email-etiquette*

8 Breathing Exercises for Anxiety You Can Try Right Now
*https://www.healthline.com/health/breathing-exercises-for-anxiety*

Improving Group Dynamics with
Facilitator-Led Group Conversations
*https://lgpress.clemson.edu/publication/improving-group-dynami-cs-with-facilitator-led-group-conversations/*